EYES *Without* A FACE

A true story of survival from emotional, sexual and physical abuse

SAMUEL P. HOLLOWAY III

THREE
PUBLISHING

Visit my website at

www.SamuelHolloway3.com

Third Printing

ISBN: 978-0-6157-0468-5

10 9 8 7 6 5 4 3 2 1

DEDICATION

I dedicate this book to my best friend, the late TyKeisha LeNora Kelly. She showed me with GOD all things are possible.

I also dedicate this book and my mission to anyone who has been abused. GOD is always in control. I am a living witness.

ACKNOWLEDGEMENTS

First and foremost, I would like to thank GOD. I know that without GOD in my life, none of this would have been possible. When one door closes, a window will always open.

Writing this book has helped me move on with my life and forgive those who have caused me pain. I pray that this book will start the healing process that I so desperately seek. I pray that this book will build a bridge for me between my mother and my father. I acknowledge the love and support of my parents.

I would like to thank my circle of family and friends for supporting me and standing by me in writing this book.

I want to give special thanks to Shantel Floyd, Kinyacta Milton, Felicia Edmond, Jessica Thao, Michelle Jarvis, Justin Kelly, and Damien Snowden for their input on this book.

Extra special thanks to my sister, LaShenia Theresa Greene, and Wilhelmina Hampton Smith, my friend and first publisher who guided me on this journey.

I also thank GOD for sending my editors, Katrice Hatten and Terrance Kelly, and my graphic designer, Jessica Godbee, into my life. They made it happen, even when I wanted to give up.

TABLE OF CONTENTS

PROLOGUE

As I laid there in fetal position with my asshole and arm bleeding, I was hurting and shaking. I was in a dark room all alone. He took something that did not belong to him. I trusted him. I was loyal to him and gave him all the praise for what he stood for to me. How could this man I called "Daddy or Father" do this to me? He had raped me and taken both my manhood and childhood. This was not like being paid for sex. He fucked me until he busted a nut and walked right out the door after he slashed my arm with the blade he carried. When I looked at my arm, I saw the white meat. I thought to myself, *How the hell did I get all the way here to Minneapolis? How is it that now I am being raped coming from DuSable Arms Apartments (the projects) in Gary, Indiana?* I remember crying hysterically before passing out.

CHAPTER ONE

THE MOVE TO MINNESOTA

It was early morning and the birds were chirping. The sun still snoozing soundly under the horizon, it was literally a cold, dark morning, December 22, 1998. For me it was BRIGHT and NEW. It had been about three months since my trip to Minnesota, and I was finally moving. Blockbuster transferred me to a location down the street from my brother's house, and I got accepted into the University of Minnesota. I couldn't wait to start my new year in a new venue with new opportunities.

I loaded all my worldly possessions in my Chevy Beretta. The driver side door still leaked in the rain or when the snow melted. My steering wheel hose was leaking, and now it had no heat. It was still the most loyal piece of junk a person could have. It ran, and that's all that mattered. I visited a couple of people before I headed out. It was ironic. Kim was the reason I even went to Minnesota, and due to last minute changes, she wasn't even moving anymore, but I was. I saw that my life was going nowhere in Gary. I knew if I stayed I would end up just like the others, in jail or dead.

I left Gary about noon-ish. Once I was on the highway, I made a promise to myself that I would never move back. I put my foot on the gas and didn't look back. I prayed, cried, and thanked GOD for the opportunity to leave Gary. Bundled up and ready for whatever the road had to offer, I drove 7½ hours with no heat into minus thirty degree weather. I knew it was better than anything I was leaving behind. I was prepared and very anxious. I listened to Whitney Houston's CD, My Love Is Your Love, the entire trip, and thought of how my life was about to change for the better.

As easy as it was for me to get to St. Paul, once I got to within the city, I got lost. I called my brother, and he directed me right down the street to his front door. (I really was lost. I promise!) I pulled up excited, nervous, anxious, curious and victorious at the same time. I had really elevated to a new level in life. I was going to be living with my brother, and that was a major deal. Growing up in Gary was hard. Having a gay little brother made it harder on him. Romie didn't chose to be my defender or to acknowledge that he had a gay brother. I wasn't mad at him for his decision not to claim me. I also understood that the streets of Gary were hard, and to be gay or even to associate with a "sissy/punk/faggot" would not be good. He allowed so many negative people to influence his relationship with me that it formed a huge gap between us, so I felt now would be our time to bond and really get to know each other.

******

Living in Minnesota was slowly showing me the move was worth it. School was coming along nicely. On top of that, I got along with my brother and his family without incident and was even doing a little traveling. I was young and eager to try many new things. So in March when my friend Jonathan, a flight attendant, planned a trip to fly some of his friends to Hawaii, I was packed before he finished asking me to go. We could bring someone, so I brought my friend Arthur from Gary. He was the first straight boy I started kicking it with. We attended Indiana University together, and he was real cool. I figured since everyone was going with a lover, and I didn't have one and didn't even want one, he would be a good friend to chill with while everyone else was "booed up."

I drove to Gary to pick up Arthur and Keisha, Jonathan's best friend, and her girlfriend. We drove to Chicago Midway Airport and left for Hawaii. Jonathan and the others lived in Las Vegas, so they met us in Hawaii.

This was only my second time flying. I had never been out of the continental United States before, so I was excited but somewhat nervous at the same time. Furthermore, because Jonathan was the greatest, this vacation was basically free, $50 round trip with his buddy passes! I mean $50 for a week in paradise, who could ask for anything more? Needless to say, my nerves settled.

When we landed, I couldn't believe my eyes. This was a long way from Gary, Indiana. The air was so crisp and smelled pretty. Flowers, trees, mountains, the ocean, the scenery was all so beautiful to me. Our accommodations were nothing less than spectacular; we stayed at the Hilton Inn Suites, right on the beach. The water was beautiful. You could see right through it. It was warm, and everyone looked like they were having so much fun swimming and playing. I was too afraid to get in all the way, so I sat at the shore and just watched them. I was in Hawaii, BITCH! I didn't care if I got in the water or not.

Our last night in Hawaii over dinner Jonathan told us it was time to live, and we were about to do it big. He said as long as he was a flight attendant, we were going to travel, and see the world for free. I was game! I really hadn't been anywhere except Gary,

Chicago, Minnesota, and now Hawaii. I was ready to see the rest of the world!

******

A long and much less exciting flight home dropped me back into my reality—my job and school. Life went on as usual. Then just as I was starting to really settle in and feel good about my new surroundings, I was pulled out of class and my whole situation took a dramatic change. I was notified that I was unable to receive financial aid because I was an out of state resident. I had to pay $5,000 cash or dropout. I dropped out. I was upset for a few days, but I figured I couldn't let it get the best of me. I continued to work at Blockbuster, and picked up a second job at a gas station, as a means to try and raise the money to pay for school.

One night at the gas station a woman came in. She was thick with brown skin, short hair and super friendly. She instantly connected with me. She told me to call her Ms. Ganet, and said she would love for me to meet her son because she thought we would have a lot in common. I was still fairly new to the area, so I decided it couldn't hurt and gave her my number. A couple days passed when she called and invited me over for dinner. About mid-evening, I headed towards downtown St. Paul where she stayed in this nice apartment complex. The apartment was immaculate. It had beautiful amenities like stainless steel appliances, granite counter tops, hardwood floors and a big balcony with a beautiful view of downtown St. Paul. NICE!

Ms. Ganet's son, Shabastion, didn't live with her, so we went downstairs to meet him. He pulled up in a red convertible BMW. I was stunned, shocked and very impressed. He was gorgeous, and by far the sexiest guy I had seen in Minnesota up to this point.

He was a redbone, 19 years old, about 5'8" and 170 lbs. He had an amazing athletic build and rocking a dark Caesar haircut. I mean, he was really hot and apparently doing very well for himself. Small talk over dinner led to Shabastion and I excusing ourselves to the balcony to talk more openly. I could not wait to find out where he worked, and what kind of money he was making that enabled him to drive a BMW and live in his own place at 19. He got the biggest kick out of watching me manage my curiosity. He then told me he was a male escort. My eyebrows went straight up. I was definitely intrigued. I felt since he was open enough to tell me his profession that I could confide in him as well. I began to explain my money issues and how I got kicked out of school. I also told him about my living situation and that I was ready to be on my own. We had a great laugh over the Beretta. (I still love my car!) He filled me in a little on the way everything worked. He told me how appointments got made, what some did and others didn't. Then he told me that he could get me in and gave me a number to call. He told me to drop his name. I thought about it again and decided I was going to try it. Fuck working two jobs, I'm going to use my body to get what I want and what I need.

I made the call, mentioned Shabastion's name, and scheduled a time to meet with "Boss." Seriously, that was his name. That is the name that I know him by to this day. We met at a penthouse in downtown Minneapolis, It was amazing! It had the opulence of a hotel lobby in South Beach, but the classic finesse of a condo on New York's Upper West Side. The place had dark hardwood floors, lush white carpet, and a state of the art kitchen with two refrigerators.

Boss invited me to sit down. He started the conversation without hesitation. He assured me that everything would be okay and that he would take me under his wing. He said it was imperative that I follow his directions, and honor four key rules:

1. Never go behind his back and try to get one of his clients,
2. Always have security with me on my runs,
3. Never get too wasted, so I can't perform or run the risk of miscounting the money,
4. Never, EVER, cross him.

Boss instantly took an interest in me after hearing that I wanted to become an escort. Now I realize he really didn't care why. The reason was the same for all of us. MONEY!

The next thing we talked about was my pay. I needed to know that it was worth it to actually sell my body. He broke it down just like this. He let me know that I would be meeting with high paying clients who were married and would live all over the world but mostly in the Minneapolis St. Paul, Minnesota area.

The split started at 60/40 his way. I was to fuck anyone that he scheduled me to meet. We would only meet at hotels across the Twin Cities. A security guard would take me to the venue and bring me back to the Boss' house to settle up the money. This would happen four to five days per week. Oral sex paid out $600 dollars per hour. Meaning he got $400, then I would get $200. Sex, if I was being fucked by a man, started at $1,000 per hour. He would get $600, and I would get $400. If I was fucking the man, it was $1,200 per hour. He would get $700, and I would get $500. If my client was a woman, the rate would start at $1500 per hour. He got $900, and I would get $600.

I think that Boss felt like he could exploit me because of my situation. It may have seemed that Boss had all of the power, but really he did not. You see, I didn't have shit to lose at that moment. I decided I was going to counter Boss's offer, and tell him that the 60/40 split had to be reversed. I explained what I brought to the table, and I was looking to get paid what I was worth. I sold him on the fact that I was a hard worker with a 10-inch dick; would fuck women and men, and work at least five days per week. He agreed to my terms, and I started immediately.

I got a call that my first shift would start around 2am. I arrived at the Boss' house. Immediately I was briefed about my trick and offered weed and alcohol. Boss always had "Kush" and an assortment of the best vodkas and tequilas on the market to get us primed for duty. I took four shots and smoked a full blunt before the security guard and I rode out to Mystic Lake Casino where my first client, a 38 year old white man, was waiting on me. Based on his picture, he was not exceptional in the looks department, but not TUTFFM (too ugly to fuck for money).

His request stated that he wanted to fuck me, and he wanted oral sex. I ran the numbers in my head. That was a total of $1600 for just an hour. For two hours it would be $3200. I was going to automatically get $1000 tonight, and I knew I could make that $2000. Afterwards, we split the money. I walked to the door and my heart was pounding. I was nervous as shit, but I was in the "zone." I was so high and buzzed that I just had one thing on my mind. Money. I knocked on the door, and he opened it right away. The room was lit as I requested because I needed to see everything on him from head to toe before I did anything. He was already naked. He was cute, and he had a nice body. He appeared to be about 6'3 about 210 pounds solid with blond hair, blue eyes and a 7-inch dick. He was going to be perfect for my first job. He was a realtor. He told me that I was fine and sexy and he wanted us to have a long-term thing if everything was to his liking.

He also said the magic word. TIPS. We got to keep all the tips, so I knew I had to work it BABY! And I did. I did everything that he wanted which was oral sex and sex.

After the night was over, I walked out with my part being $2500. I got paid a total of $3200 for the job and $500 for my tip. I did what I had to do for two hours. As I walked out the hotel room door, I felt good, and I felt bad. I felt good because I could pay all my bills in advance if I wanted to, and do whatever else I needed. I finally had enough money to live, and I managed to make it in just one night. Then I felt bad because I just had sex with a married man with children for money. But I didn't care as I felt that money in my back pocket. I figured I had done this before in my past anyway without getting paid as much, but now I was getting paid a lot. The money numbed my bad feelings, and all I could think of was making more money. I got back in the car. The security guard and I drove back to the Boss' house. After that night, I knew it was on and popping. I was hooked. When I pulled out the cash, Boss' eyes got really big. He looked like, *what the fuck?* He knew exactly how much he was getting paid.

When I got back to my brother's house it was late. I was feeling good. I had a pocket full of money, and for the first time I knew that I was soon to be on my own.

CHAPTER TWO

ON MY OWN

West St. Paul Apartments was my kind of place. It had the newest appliances, large windows, a balcony and space of my own. Yes! March 1, 2001, was the day I truly was on my own. I was "escorting" more than ever and had become Boss' number one dude. I had even become his most requested "trick".

However, as with my life, something good is always followed by something bad. My Uncle Kenny was being admitted into the hospital. Before my uncle was admitted, he suggested I should get an apartment with Nina, his 19-year old daughter conceived outside of his marriage. He felt like she needed to be out on her own, but with a little oversight. I knew what he really wanted was to make sure that she would be taken care of after he passed. Once Uncle Kenny was in the hospital, she really began to be treated like the stepchild. Nina was like my little sister, so I had to make sure she was okay. It was important for me to uphold my uncle's wishes.

After five years of battling cancer, Uncle Kenny was truly laying on his death bed. Thankfully, he was surrounded by his close friends and family that included seven of his ten children. He got the chance to speak to his mother, brother, sisters, children, grandchildren, some nieces, nephews, and friends. Uncle Kenny and I had a terrible relationship during the course of my childhood. He was mean and cold to me. Like some of the others in my family, he taunted me for being gay. Thankfully, it did not last, and the one memory that I will always cherish is the day he apologized to me.

******

I was 16-years old when my grandfather died. We were at my aunt's house for the repast after his funeral. Uncle Kenny asked if he could speak to me alone. I said okay, and we stepped outside. Before the door could close behind us, my uncle began to cry. My grandfather just died, so I didn't think it was strange until he started speaking. He told me how sorry he was for all the wrong that he had done to me. I stood there completely confused. I didn't know what he was talking about. You see, when you are a child in an abusive family, at a certain point abusive behavior becomes normal behavior. I tried to be assuring and compassionate. I comforted my uncle telling him that everything was going to be okay. I didn't know then what his sobs and apologies were all about, but I would soon find out.

We sat with Uncle Kenny to give him comfort. He was in and out of consciousness. Most times he was crying because he was in pain that we could not imagine. He was hooked to IVs, and could not eat or drink. His mouth had to be swabbed when he was thirsty because of the pain from swallowing.

Uncle Kenny wanted our family to stay together. He spent his last days making that clear to everyone. He told the family to accept me. He begged them not to knock me down but to support me and love me. The look on his face and the tone in his voice, stern yet apologetic, was so sincere. Whenever I think about it, it's like I'm in that room listening to it for the first time. What he stated to me alone is the reason I am who I am today. I am so thankful and blessed that GOD allowed my uncle to live, so I could hear what he told me. It made an everlasting difference in my life going forward.

******

April 7th, 2001, Uncle Kenny said something that shocked everyone. "Tomorrow, my father is coming to take me home," he said. On April 8, 2001, exactly five years after my grandfather passed, Uncle Kenny died. It was so devastating to watch him just vanish before my eyes, but my grandfather had indeed come to take him home. My brother Romie got arrested the very next day after Uncle Kenny died. He caught a drug charge with possession of a weapon. He was convicted and spent the next 3½ years in prison. Romie and I were not talking, but I didn't want my brother to be in jail. He put me out of his house six months after I moved in because his wife accused me of wearing her sanitary napkins.

******

All the devastation around me landed me back on a plane headed to Jonathan's house in Baltimore, Maryland, where he had recently relocated. We were like best friends, and I confided in him. We had no sexual relationship at all. He was a strong shoulder when I needed one, just as I was for him. Thanks to him, I was a regular face around Northwest Airlines and was regularly upgraded to First Class without asking. This was truly a luxury that I took advantage of and all of the benefits that came with it. When I landed, I took in the deepest breath I could. Baltimore was, by far, still one of my least favorite cities, but it wasn't Minnesota. That's all that mattered.

Jonathan and I never stayed in Baltimore when I went to visit, and this trip was no different. Jonathan wanted to drive to Philly, so we did. Philly is not much of a city, but the downtown district is nice. It was a nice evening, and we were walking the main street when this guy walked up and grabbed my arm. I was shocked, to say the least, but when I turned around I was very intrigued. He was definitely not black. His skin was white but he had thick, black, curly hair, so he couldn't have been white. He stood about 5'9, working a fitted wife beater that covered a well-defined body, and he had a smile that could melt the sun.

"Excuse me, are you two together?" he asked.

His voice was sexy too, but I couldn't let him see how open I was. So in a sarcastic tone with a slight smile, I replied, "If we were, that would have just been so disrespectful; you coming and grabbing me like that."

He in turn looked me right in the eye and asked again, "Are you together?"

I quickly said, "No. this is my best friend. And you are?"

"Wilton. I live in D.C. I am just visiting Philly for the weekend. Now can I get your name?"

I stared Wilton up and down. He was gorgeous, and he was interested in me. Of course he could get my name.

"Robert, nice to meet you" I answered. "I'm also visiting for the weekend from Minnesota."

We stepped to the side and continued our conversation. He was 28, black and Italian, had a car and was a manager for AT&T. The best thing was that he was bisexual. That is what attracted me to him. We exchanged numbers, and he asked if he was really going to see me again. I told him I lived in Minnesota, and that was up to him. He said if I was okay with it that he would like to fly me to DC the following weekend. Yes. He was fine, but I told him that that was something I had to think about. He said he could respect that, and he'd call me later. We went our separate ways.

I thought of him the entire ride back to Baltimore. If he was going to fly me out to D.C. from Minnesota, he had to have money. I was still in money-making mode, so I only messed around with men that had money. He was perfect from the outside—very masculine, extremely handsome, and had a nice physique. He had what I wanted from a man. Since I experienced sex at an early age and was having sex for money, there was no passion or meaning behind it or anymore. All of my friends were either in a relationship or just getting out of one. I'd never been in a relationship, and I wanted to know what that felt like. Plus, I wanted that masculine feeling and touch around me. Not getting my hopes too high, I just decided we would see where it went.

******

Jonathan planned another trip in May to go to Texas Splash, which is Gay Pride in Galveston, Texas. This would be my first time in Texas, and I would be near the beach. I couldn't wait. We met up at the airport, got our rental car and headed to the hotel right off the beach front. I was from the projects. This was so far from my reality. I was traveling like a millionaire staying in amazing hotels and meeting beautiful people. I never would've imagined this, but I loved every minute of it.

The highlight of the weekend was Wilton. He had already planned to go before we met, so it was perfect. We spent our first night together, and it was amazing. I mean, it was so good we named it!

Pride was hot, hot, hot, and extra hot! Jonathan left with his friend, but I was fine with that because Wilton was all over me. It was over 100 degrees, so we spent the day together at the beach. I felt so good being with him. I made a comment about the sand being hot as hell and was taken aback when he picked me up and carried me on his shoulders. The gays were out. I felt comfortable and in my zone. Worries of life were so far from my mind. I was enjoying myself and having an amazing time!

Sunday morning, Jonathan and I rode around and saw Galveston and the cities outside of Galveston. It was beautiful but was way too hot for me. We finished our drive with a visit to Jonathan's family in Houston. When we got back to Galveston, I said my goodbyes to Wilton. He and his friend were leaving that night because he had to work in the morning. I, on the other hand, was off Monday, so we were leaving the next morning.

Wilton called immediately after I got home just like he said he would. He asked for my information, so he could book me a flight. I gave it to him, and he emailed me the flight confirmation. For the next three months, we had a whirlwind romance. I was living a life far from DuSable Arms Projects. I was making more money than I cared to count, traveling and living well, I thought I was happy.

CHAPTER THREE

INVASION OF PRIVACY

The "Gay 90s" club was still the most popular and always live gay club in Minnesota, and by August I was what you may consider single. But to be honest, I was never really taken. My relationship with Wilton was never really committed or defined. Our weekend rendezvous started to become fewer and farther between. Before long, I found myself single and available. I started hanging out at the club a lot. I wasn't going to ruin my summer because of a boy.

I was always with Shabastion and ready to have a good time. Shabastion was my best friend at this point. He was still in the top 10 on Minnesota's "finest men" list, but he was my closest gay friend in every way. I knew with him my secrets were safely kept.

One fun-filled night of dancing and drinking, Shabastion and I got split up. The club was crazy packed. Boys everywhere!! I knew Shabastion could handle himself, and I'd find him by night's end. I decided to go upstairs to the drag show. On the way up, I ran into a guy about 6'3" and a solid 280 pounds of muscle. He was bald with a goatee and large brown eyes. His voice was unbelievably deep. His feet must have been a size thirteen. I always check out a man's feet. He was a monster-sized man, and ironically he was very friendly. He flirted with me and asked my name. I was not attracted to him at first sight, and I told him that.

He said his name was Bernard. He was one of the bouncers there. That explained his size. He was gay and single. I let him know I was not interested. He seemed like a very cool person to be friends with. I told him he seemed like the perfect "Gay Father" figure, and he laughed. After my uncle passed and with Romie in jail, I was missing a male to talk straight with. We exchanged numbers just as Shabastion was walking up. Immediately Shabastion began to ask questions about whom was I giving my number to? I explained to him what I thought about Bernard as we walked away, and that was that.

A couple of weeks passed before Bernard called me. We ended up talking for hours. It's funny how you can just be so open with some people. He made me feel comfortable. I learned a lot about him that night. He had just moved to Minnesota from Arkansas and stayed nearby with his sister in Roseville. He was forty-six years old with two children, a boy and a girl. He told me how he lived his life on the "down low" and made the decision to fully come out as gay. He also mentioned he was in the process of getting a divorce, and that's why he made the move to Minnesota. I told him about my travels and my friends. I didn't really say anything about my mom or brother because at the moment it was all negative.

We spoke a lot after that, but our conversations were not really about anything significant. I was still a busy boy. I was working and traveling a lot. The friendship was fine with me because I had money and fun on my mind.

******

September 12 was fast-approaching. Jonathan and I were going to Cancun for his birthday. I met him in Chicago and we flew out together from there. His friends from Vegas met us in Cancun.

Our hotel was right on the beach, as usual, but this time Jonathan went all out. We stayed in a penthouse suite with a magnificent city view. There was a Jacuzzi tub on the balcony, along with exotic tropical plants and flowers. We drank in the streets, walked on the beach and really relaxed. The water was green and nasty, but that was fine because I had no intention of getting in it anyway.

It was Labor Day week and the crowd was live. There was a party every night and places to chill and put your feet up. We had an amazing time.

The morning before we were set to leave, someone called Jonathan's phone relentlessly. I wanted to get up and throw it, but I was so tired and my head was throbbing. I couldn't get out of the bed, so I tuned it out. He finally answered the phone, and next I heard a loud thud. He screamed, "WHAT?!" He ran to turn on the TV. The first thing I see was a plane crashing into one of the Twin Towers. We started screaming and crying once we realized the image was the same on every channel. Two planes had deliberately been flown into the Twin Towers and one into the Pentagon. We were being attacked. I didn't know what to think. I opened the door to the hotel room, and people were running and crying. I was stuck and confused. Were they going to attack us? I was so scared.

Jonathan broke my daze when he started yelling, "Robert, get your shit and pack! We have to go now! They're going to start grounding flights." I knew that he knew what he was talking about and hurried and started packing. My hands were shaking. I was still trying to digest all that was happening. Clothes and shoes in our suitcases, we ran out into the hotel hall, which was full of emotion and bustle, to try and get a cab. We didn't even bother to check out or do a double-check of the hotel to see if we had left anything. Still in our pajamas, we were on our way to the airport hoping we'd get there before the flights were grounded.

The airport was a complete disaster. I think every tourist in Mexico was trying to get home. Lines were wrapped about the airport. Everyone wanted to be heard. Everyone's story and reason was more important than the next person's. The place was in a complete state of panic. People were screaming, hollering, crying and fainting. It was sad. I couldn't even stop the tears falling from my eyes.

All flights had been delayed, and then they grounded all flights into the U.S. There was a bigger problem. If we changed our flights, we would have to pay for a ticket, and that was not going to be cheap. We needed to get to California. That was going to be our safe haven. There were no flights straight to California, but because we could fly around Mexico, we could get several different flights that would eventually land us in California. The flights were a little more than $600 a piece, and that ONLY got us to California. My money was in an online account, and all the information pertaining to it was it was at home, in Minneapolis, locked up. I didn't know what we were going to do.

We spent a very uncomfortable night in the airport and left the next day because we couldn't afford the flight. Standby still wasn't an option. We got a cab back to the hotel and learned there were no available rooms. We got on the bus and rode around Cancun searching for a hotel. I knew that this was not how Jonathan planned to spend his birthday. I felt for him. We had to come up with a plan and quick. We didn't intend to stay in Cancun pass

September 12th, so now we would have to spend more money on a room and still get the money together to get a ticket out of Mexico.

We finally found a hotel that wasn't trying to make as much as possible off of the terrorist attacks in the U.S. and decided that we should call our parents to ask for the money. The next morning my mother met Jonathan's mother, and they wired us the money that we needed. We went back to the airport and purchased four different tickets to get back stateside.

With the money our parents sent and a little help from our credit cards, we were on our way. Our final flight delivered us to a city outside of Tijuana, Mexico where we walked to customs to get to the border of California. My sister LaShenia met us at the gate, and we went back to her house. I was so grateful. It took two hours to drive back to her house, but that was fine. I was no longer in Mexico. We stayed at LaShenia's just for a night. The ban was lifted on the 14th, and we hopped on a plane towards home. I was nervous, but I knew that I would be okay. I just had to keep my faith.

By the time I got home, President Bush had declared war and was sending troops to Afghanistan. I was scared to fly after that for a minute. I held off on flying for almost a year. I will never forget that ordeal. My heart will forever go out to the families and victims of September 11.

******

Everyone was asking about my experience, but not so surprisingly my mother really didn't seem to care. She told me she wanted her money back and to talk to her when I had it. Sometimes I just couldn't believe her. She went back and forth to Romie's trial but never even bothered to come see my place. He was facing ten years for a gun and drug possession. He was my mother's favorite person in the world, and she wanted to make sure he did as little time as possible. With her help, the lawyer got Romie's charges reduced to three and a half years in prison.

After the trial was complete, she started speaking to me again. She was so finicky. She said she was happy I was making it and was consistently asking if she could do anything to help with the new apartment. I suggested blinds for the living room. Just like my mother, always on time, in November the blinds arrived. As strong and as strapping as I am, hanging blinds is not something that comes natural to me. After I scattered all the pieces across the living room floor and looked at the directions, I didn't even want to try anymore. I placed everything back in the box and set it against the wall neatly.

A couple nights later while talking to Bernard, I told him about my failed attempt at blind hanging and explained that's just one of the reasons I should not do manual labor. He laughed then offered to come over before he went to the gym that weekend to put them up. I told him then that I was strapped for cash because I was saving for something. He said that was fine, and it wouldn't be a problem. He would be doing his son a favor, he added.

Around 2:00am the next morning, I dreamed that someone was trying to kill me. I couldn't get away fast enough. I felt like I was running in slow motion, but I made it. My heart was pounding, and my body was sweating. I sat up and cried. Ironically, that would be one of the many unpleasant and vivid dreams to come.

The next morning it was cold outside. The scenery was beautiful from my third floor balcony. Everything was covered in white. It was the beginning of November. We must have just had a fresh snowfall in the middle of the night. The brightness along with the sunshine made the house so full of light. Everything seemed so picture perfect. I was living my dreams finally. I had my own place after struggling for the last year, and I was able to breathe, relax and explore.

Bernard arrived around 1:00 pm. I took him on a tour of my apartment. I was so proud of it. We talked a little, and he seemed like the perfect "Gay Father." After he put the blinds up, which only took about twenty minutes; he began to look around very suspiciously. His entire demeanor changed, and he was not the pleasant man I had been talking with all this time. His body seemed to bulk up like the Incredible Hulk. His eyes had that mean look in them like I had said something that offended him. He then began to hover over me and began talking.

"How was I going to pay him for his services?"

Slightly annoyed I replied, "I told you I'm strapped for cash, but if you want it that bad, I will go to an ATM."

In a usually calm voice he replied, "I don't want your money. You can pay me with some ass!"

Dumbfounded and taken aback, I started backing away from the couch. "I'm cool on that. I looked at you in a different way," I added. "I'm not interested in you on that level."

I was kicking and punching as he grabbed me by my neck. He picked me up and carried me into my own bedroom. I couldn't get out of his arms. He threw me on top of the bed, and we tussled until I couldn't fight him anymore.

I was in an unimaginable place. He ripped my shorts and boxers off and spat on his hand to wet his penis. Like a completely different person with no care or concern he rammed his penis into me and began raping me. I was laying there crying, totally defenseless. I tried screaming out for help and for him to put a condom on at the very least. He covered my mouth and continued to rape me.

I could feel his semen enter my body when he was finally done. He pulled up his pants and pulled a switchblade from his pocket. Threatening me not to tell anyone, he slashed my arm with the blade and simply walked out the door.

As I lay in my bed paralyzed and bloody from the traumatic experience that I had just gone through, I started to have flashbacks about my past. I must have fainted because as I awoke, I was laying in a pool of blood from both ends. I got up and ran to the bathroom where I began to vomit. I had blood everywhere. My bedroom looked like a war zone. I ran some warm bath water, got in the tub and laid there crying. Death seemed like the perfect option at that moment, but I thought, "How could I take my own life when, even in that horrible moment, someone else had just spared mine?" I was so displaced. Did he think about killing me? He could have, and no one would have known. But then again, maybe he left me there to ponder how it was so easy for him to violate me and get away with it. Was that the reason he spared my life?

I felt embarrassed and ashamed. I felt dirty. He left a smell on me that wasn't coming off. A sharp jolt in my arm made me remember the cut. It was a healthy slice, long and deep. This was going to be a scar I would have to carry forever. An even sharper pain in my ass shook me out of that daze. It was burning terribly. All I could do was cry.

Hurting and confused with a million questions running through my head, I began to ponder. *How could I let this happen to me? What would I do next? Would I tell anybody that I had just been raped? Can a man get raped?* These thoughts, and more, ran through my head as I lay on clothes palette in my living room in fetal position trying to gather myself.

As I laid there in the darkness, the only sound was the cars driving by outside. I closed my eyes, and I wished that I was in my mother's arms. I wanted the loving mother that I had when my best friend passed away. She was there to make sure her baby boy was okay. I needed her now.

"GOD, please help me!" Then I passed out.

CHAPTER FOUR

A DREAM, A SIMPLE MEMORY

It's 3:15 am. It's very quiet in the house. I turned on my side in the top bunk. I could see the figure again. He was standing over me with huge abnormally large eyes and big hands. He was rubbing my legs first, then he went up higher until he touched my butt. He pulled my underwear down, and fingers started rubbing my butt. One hand was holding his penis, and the other rubbing me. I started crying and screamed out.

The snow and streetlights brought me back to reality. My heart was beating fast. My face was wet, and I couldn't seem to catch my breath. What was that all about? Did this really happen? I began to ask myself all kinds of questions as I rocked in my bed. The biggest question was *who the fuck was I dreaming about?* My mind was so heavy. I was a 22-year old male escort with a dead uncle, an imprisoned brother, and a temperamental mother. I had lost a lot of family being gay, and I didn't have many friends because I was in a new state and still trying to hide my sexuality. The cherry on this "nasty cake" was I am now a rape victim and keeping it a secret. I was having these very intense and terrible dreams, and I didn't know what these dreams were about.

A couple of months later, I told Nina and Shabastion about Bernard raping me. I thought that it would make me feel better, but it didn't. I was still sad, still did not want to report it and was so confused about the entire situation that I just tried to bury it. Something was different though.

Big buck teeth—sitting at a fold-away table with Romie—plates in front of us—mom in living room on the checkered green and white sofa looking sad and talking to her husband. Why weren't they eating? Romie said, "Shut up!" The refrigerator only had condiments, jelly, water, butter and baking soda in it. Where is the food? The refrigerator turned into a Christmas tree. These gifts suck! Socks, underwear and t-shirts? Where are the toys? Heavy snowfall. Wait for me Romie!!!! We both had tan coats with hoods. We could have been twins. The sled was so fast. Pop on the back of the head. You are such a dummy getting five D's. But Grandma, Troy got F's! Grandma is in the store buying Troy a game.

I shot straight up gasping for air. These were things I remembered. Unlike the first couple of dreams, I wasn't sad when I woke up. I was angry and confused. The bullshit I remembered sometimes just annoyed the hell out of me. From that night forward the dreams/memories, more so nightmares, kept coming. Night after night I was waking up annoyed and CONFUSED or in cold sweats and crying.

******

I hadn't been to the club in months fearing I would see Bernard. He never called me after that night, and I never saw him again. Shabastion suggested I go to the club and face him to put it behind me. I thought that was the dumbest idea, but I couldn't keep living in this bubble. It was taking a toll on my life, both personally and professionally. I was terrified the night we went to the club. We walked to the entrance, and there he was. Bernard stood there with a smile so wide you could see his back teeth. He reached out to me and asked why I hadn't called him. My heart started beating rapidly. My palms were sweating, and I wanted to scream, "You bastard! You rapped me!" Instead, I walked right pass him and into the club.

What Bernard didn't know was we'd done an investigating and found out he had a boyfriend. Shabastion, being the bitch that he is, found out that Bernard's boyfriend was and spotted him in the club. He told the boy what Bernard did to me; bad idea. The boy blew up and started accusing me of wanting Bernard. Before I knew it, we were outside in the parking lot.

Shabastion and the boy were arguing. I was so scared, I pleaded with Shabastion for us to leave. This did not make me feel any better about the situation. As we were walking away, the boy screamed, "Well, since your fucking him, did you know he had AIDS?"

I could have passed out and died. My heart hit the floor, and I started crying. If the rape wasn't enough, now I had this to think about. My entire body went limp. Shabastion grabbed me, and I realized a crowd had formed around us. The cops were headed our way, so we hustled towards the car and left. Shabastion told me if I needed him to go to the clinic with me that he would. We went the next day.

My results came back. HIV negative. Praise GOD!

******

Look at how pretty I am. Girl clothes make me feel so connected with myself. You stupid ass nigga! (Punch!)Fuck you out here walking around like that?! (Punch! Punch! Punch!) My eye started burning.

Punch! Punch! Punch! Relentless-Punch! Punch! Punch, I touched my lip.

OMG, ROMIE, STOP!!!!!!!!!! I screamed out as I jolted out of my sleep grabbing my eye. My bed was wet from sweating, and my covers were all balled up like I was fighting someone. All these dreams were starting to drive me crazy. Was I holding in something? What was the purpose? Why had these dreams started? They were so real that I could vomit. Some were easy to remember while others stumped me. I just laid there and thought for a long time before I eventually fell back asleep.

******

March 2002 couldn't have come fast enough. I figured the only reason I was having the dreams was because I was still in that apartment. I was ready to get out. Nina and I found a two-story European style townhome. I had the furniture, so moving in and getting settled was not a problem. I figured the new place would bring positive energy.

Nina and I got along fine. She respected my privacy. I respected hers. We lived happily ever after—well, close enough anyway.

I was forced into the red two-door car. I was lying down being taken away, more like kidnapped. Riding, all I could see were the tops of tin buildings with smoke coming out. The car turned and my body jerked. There was only sky. Someone grabs me by my arm. It was those big eyes again. They were eyes without a face. The person was tall. The strong arm began dangling me over unreflective green water, screaming, "Tell, and I'll kill you!" over and over. My mom came rushing pass me in the house. I could hear her ruffling around in the other room. She came back in the room and began to hit me over and

27

over with a shower rod unmercifully. Then she stops and with an evil grin kicks me with a black stiletto.

Oh my GOD! My knee was throbbing. My face was wet again. This was the third consecutive night I woke up at 3:30am, and my bed was like a swimming pool. I was drenched, and this time I was cryingso loud that Nina ran into my room to check on me and asked what was wrong. I began to tell her about my dreams. I explained how I always dreamt but never like this, and these particular dreams started coming more frequently after the rape. She tried to ensure me that I was only dreaming. I didn't want to believe that they were true but what else was there? Were these really just dreams or simple memories?

CHAPTER FIVE

INNOCENCE TAKEN AWAY

I guess you can say that I had a serious case of memory repression. In fact, I didn't remember much of my childhood. I knew that it wasn't raspberries and snow cones, but I didn't think it was bad. My mother and I always fought and bickered, but the things I learned completely shocked me. There were several others that I disliked. I thought it was just because they never agreed with my lifestyle choice.

My mother, the middle child of six, was the black sheep, so it only seemed natural that one of her children would follow suit. She had naturally silky, curly, reddish hair and a shape any woman would kill for. It was her personality that turned off the men. You could give her anything her heart desired, but if she was mad, she turned evil. No one would dare to be around her during that time.

My brother Romie, the oldest of my mothers' three children, was hardly around, but when he was, he loved to put his hands on me. He hit and kicked me and called me names. I don't ever remember my brother being nice to me as a child. He was always cruel and never showed me any type of affection. I thought it was going to be different once I moved with him, but that wasn't the case. We were closer but still not friends.

******

Second in command was Uncle Kenny. He was crueler than my brother. Unlike my brother, he never put his hands on me. He was verbally abusive. Uncle Kenny called me names like, "faggot" and "sissy." Those names were painful and they tore me apart. Uncle Kenny used to force my brother to fight me because he said I needed a backbone. Of course, Romie would beat the hell out of me. I do remember the way that my body would cringe as a child when he was present. He sent chills down my spine.

******

Finally, after repeatedly questioning myself and agonizing over the validity of my dreams, I decided to start asking questions. One night I placed a call to my mother while Nina sat on the foot of my bed. It was a call I will never forget. With every ring, I grew a little more nervous. My leg was shaking. I was fighting back tears. My heart was pounding.

"Hello," she sounded calm enough for this conversation, I thought.

"Hey Ma, you busy? Got time to talk?" I was really nervous. Nina kept telling me to calm down, but I was already caught.

"What's wrong lil' Robert? You sound sick or something?" she asked, which only made me more nervous.

"Ma, I've been having these dreams..." I explained the dreams, especially the ones with the big-eyed man. I asked her if anything sounded familiar. In the coldest, harshest voice she replied, "That was something that I buried, and I wish you would bury it too."

I began to cry uncontrollably, and I just hung up the phone. It was real. These dreams were actually memories. I had been molested!

******

There was never any time to just be with myself. I was coping with being raped as an adult, molested as a child, the tarnished relationship between my mother and these intense nightmares, death, being openly gay, my brother being locked up, and my nieces were coming to live with Nina and me.

In the summer of 2002, I got a call from Rachel, the mother of one of Romie's babies. She had another child and needed some help. Thinking of myself last, I was there to step in and show them their father's side of the family was there if ever they needed. This would be a decision that would change my life dramatically.

I decided to stop the male escort service. I had done it for two years and had enough money saved up for a stormy day or month, so I knew I would be okay. I also sold the Neon because I would need something bigger. I got a midnight blue 2000 Pontiac Grand Am with all the trimmings. There was a moon roof, fog lamps, a rear spoiler and grooved body side molding. (*What? You thought I was going to get a minivan or something?*) I also started going to counseling because I did not want to help raise the kids without learning how to handle what I was personally going through. I knew I couldn't do counseling alone based on the fact that I didn't remember much, but I was privy to what I learned via my dreams. Getting my mother's help was somewhat out of the question. I was hoping someone else would know something that would help.

I started getting my nieces every other weekend, and it was fun. I was slowly getting out of the escort business, and it gave me time to do "healthy" things I enjoyed. There was always something going on within our family. Felicia loved to cook. She was damn good at it too!

Aunt Teresa's house was the main spot now that Uncle Kenny was gone. She held the family together after he passed. No matter what was going on, Aunt Teresa was in the middle of it. Sometimes it helped. Sometimes it didn't, but she always let everyone know right was right and wrong was wrong. No matter what, we are family, and we only have each other.

As the dreams poured in, I cried out for answers. I was calling people every day. I called my mother, Aunt Sylvia, Aunt Teresa, Aunt Denise, and my dad. All of them provided some kind of insight, but surprisingly it was my mother that helped put the puzzle in my head completely together.

She finally wanted to bury the hatchet. I was happy because I wanted answers. I needed answers. Then a couple days before my 23rd birthday I received a packet from my mother filled with papers. There were things I had not seen in years or simply did not remember. She had almost every report card, my dental records, some pictures that I drew and colored from elementary school, a letter and a business card—*a letter and a business card?*

11-28-2001

Habakkuk 2:2-3

> *And Jehovah proceeded to answer me and to say: write down the vision, and set it out plainly upon tablets, in order that the one reading aloud from it may do so fluently. For the vision is yet for the appointed time. It keeps pointing*

to the end, and it will not tell a lie. Even if it should delay, keep in expectation of it. For it will, without fail, come true. It will not be late. Thank you Jehovah for giving Robert T. Edmond the strength and sound mind to excel in all that he does. Give him the wisdom of understanding. Help him to endure and overcome any and all negativity in his life. Send your angels of protection all around his being. Protect his mind, heart and spirit from all hardships, neglect, abuse, and ugliness. I thank you, Jehovah, for helping Robert to forgive and continue to be loving, caring, understanding, and the knowledgeable person he is. I thank you for allowing him to love me, his mom.

I thank you, Jehovah, for allowing Robert to forgive me.

Love,
Mother

(This is for all the ill treatment that I have given him.)

Tears continued to pour from my eyes. I broke down. It was bittersweet. I needed that from her, but, at the same time, it hurt. These dreams were talking to me about me. They were true. There was still this card:

LT. ROBERT JACKSON
Police Supervisor
Dayton, Ohio

My head was spinning! A Police Supervisor?! What was that all about? I was molested, and then beaten by my mother and brother. No wonder I felt abandoned for so long. I had so many questions. I called my mother, she seemed open to helping me move on, so I got straight to the point, as soon as she picked up. "Hello?"

She seems "pleasant."

"Hey, Ma. I got your package," I said with a slight quiver in my voice.

"Oh, you got it?"

I was wrong she wasn't. "Yeah"

She was so off putting and in a very condescending tone she asked, "Oh, okay. You got any questions?"

Instantly irritated, I thought, *No I just called to shoot the breeze.* But instead responded, "Yeah."

There was a long pause. I was in so many dimensions at once I just asked, "Ummm, what is this card?"

"What card?" *Now she was confused?!*

"Robert Jackson. Who is that?" My leg was shaking as I held the card.

"That's the first question that comes out of your mouth? I remember the day you brought that picture home..."

Was she crazy? She must be insane. "Ummm, I asked you a question. ROBERT JACKSON?! WHO IS THAT???"

As if she didn't think I was in enough pain, she shouted, "That's him—the man that molested you?"

I just hung up the phone. Really?! She sent me a card with a name on it. I thought *HIS NAME IS ON IT with all his information* .

I was mad. I was ready to drive to Ohio to kill his ass. I called the number on the card and was told he had retired. Retired policeman? It must be nice. The next thought was to go to the Internet. I tried to *Google* his name every way imaginable, no luck. I even tried the *Yellow Pages* and the operator. Nothing!

I was in such a bad place. Everything I ever thought was one big, fat, huge, ole' ugly lie! How could I forget all of this? How could my own mother and my own brother just pretend like nothing happened?

It was so bad that I didn't want to talk to my mother, but I didn't have a choice. She had the answers to everything. I wanted them. She double confirmed I was molested then told me the case never made it to court because Robert, better known as "Bob" had a gay stepson who worked at the police station. He acted as a character witness. Without further questioning, they took Bob's word. There was no case. She also said it happened many years ago, and I should deal with it and move on with my life. She felt like asking her about what happened was making me "get off" she said and did not want to give me any more information. I couldn't believe her! I was "getting off" on my own molestation story? Who would say that to their child?

I took the information I had and went to Gary, Indiana to the police department, only to find that my statute of limitations had expired a year earlier. There was nothing I could do. Ironically, there was only one thought that came to my mind, *"why couldn't I have gotten raped a year earlier?"* If it wasn't for that bringing on the dreams, I would have probably never remembered my past.

CHAPTER SIX

EYES WITHOUT A FACE

We lived in DuSable Arms Apartments. This was a housing project that my grandfather's brother owned. We stayed in a two-bedroom unit, and my family was all around us. Aunt Sylvia lived right next door. Aunt Denise lived across the street from us. We had more family that lived on that side, as well as my great uncle and his wife. They were not the best living conditions. The bricks were falling off the building, and we had roaches.

I was 9 years old when my mother's associate Precious introduced her to Bob. He was an older man, maybe in his early fifties, tall and scary. He worked at Gary Steele Mill, and, I assume, made a lot of money because he immediately became my mother's "Sugar Daddy." Before long, he was putting groceries in the house and cooking for Romie and me. He allowed my mother to drive his red two-door Ford Tempo. He was buying her clothes, and then he bought her a new living room set. All of a sudden, this tall, old, scary looking man was living with us. My mother constantly left me home alone with him. I didn't really care for him, but he was always nice to me, or so I thought. He started off by giving me money and promising to take me to Great America Amusement

Park. My brother and friends were going, but I couldn't go because I was too young. Before long we bonded. He wasn't as scary as he looked, and he was actually really nice to me. I learned that whatever we talked about was to be kept between us because he always warned me, "Don't ever tell anybody what we talk about."

One night I woke up, looked out from the top of my bunk bed into a dark room. A small stream of light was shining through the bathroom door and Romie was lying in the bottom bunk bed snoring. I thought I saw a figure and rubbed my eyes to be sure. My mother's bedroom was across from ours, and Bob was in fact standing in our bedroom doorway naked. As my vision cleared, I realized he had had his penis in his hand. He started walking toward me, so I laid down real quick and closed my eyes. I was hoping he hadn't seen me looking at him. He came in and stood at the foot of the bed looking over me. He was really tall and had big eyes. His eyes are what stood out the most. They were so big and white like he had seen a ghost. He took the pillow from my bed in one hand and had his penis in the other. He then dropped the pillow on the floor, started rubbing my leg and then worked his way to my butt as he continued playing with himself. I lay as still as I could, I didn't want him to know I was awake. I did not know how to respond to his actions, so I didn't. When he finally left the room, I just turned over and closed my eyes as tight as I could and tried to fall back asleep.

He came into my bedroom on several different occasions. Each time he came while my brother was in the bottom bunk, and my mother was in the other room. He would come into the room and rub on me while he played with himself. Soon he got bored and went a step further. He knew I was awake and put his finger to his lips, and said, "Shhhh." My heart was pounding. I was scared out

37

of my mind. He started slowly sliding his finger in and out of my rectum. I bit down on the pillow, and my eyes filled with tears. It hurt so badly. I didn't like it. I wanted it to stop. All I could do was wonder. *Where was my mother? Why won't my brother wake up? Why is he doing this to me?*

I asked Bob once if I was bad, and if that's why he did these things to me? He told me he loved me, and that's how he showed it. He said it was our secret love, and if I told anyone he would kill me. I told him I didn't like it. That didn't matter much. It got so bad that things moved out of the bedroom at night into the day, in the living room. If we were alone, he would make me hold his penis and play with it. It was very long and hairy. It didn't smell so great either. He wanted me to start putting his penis in my mouth. He showed me first by putting mine in his. Told me never to use my teeth, and try to relax my throat, so he could get it all the way into my 10-year-old mouth.

He repeatedly told me, "If you ever say anything, I'll kill you". He said that he was being nice to me, and I should be happy. I should enjoy his love and keep our secret. So when my mom asked if Bob was touching me, I said no because I was scared. My Aunt Sylvia also asked me. I guess she thought maybe I'd be more comfortable telling her, but I wasn't. I heard Bob's voice in my head repeating over and over, "If you tell anyone, I will kill you". So I told her no, as well. I'm not sure if they approached him or not. But after that, Bob changed. I won't say it was for the better, but he did stop touching me and making me touch him, but not before he took me on a long ride. We seemed to be driving forever. He would not tell me where we were going. I was in the back seat of the car. All I could see were silver buildings. We came to an abrupt stop, and he walked around to my door and yanked me from the seat. He held me by the top of my arm and was almost dragging me down a barge overlooking green water. I didn't know what was wrong with him. I did just like he said, and told everyone nothing was going on, but he was mad—really mad. My heart was beating so fast. We stopped right at the end of the pier, he grabbed my other arm, looked me in the face and asked, "Did I tell anyone our secret?" I think I said no a hundred times. I was so scared I thought I was going to pee myself. He didn't say anything, just looked at me and in one clean swoop grabbed me by my arm and dangled me over the water. He was shouting, "If you told, this is where they would be finding your body". Pee traveled down my leg, as tears fell from my eyes. I told him over and over. I didn't tell. I wouldn't tell. I even promised. The ride home was quiet. When we got back, he was calm like nothing had even happened. He told me to clean my pissy pants and went on with his day.

By spring, I didn't know what was going on in my life. I was in school sick to my stomach. I didn't know how to respond to the things that were happening in my life. I was a child, but I was not dumb. My brother was a Black Stone gang member, and I heard about people being shot and killed by them. I knew it was possible, and I didn't want that to happen to me. I got so dizzy I vomited all over my computer in the computer lab. My fourth grade teachers, Mrs. Broughton and Ms. Anderson, took me to the nurse's office and called my mother. While sitting there, my third grade teacher, Mrs. Broom, asked me what was wrong and I told her what had been happening to me. She asked me if I was telling the truth, and I started crying and told her yes. I was really scared.

By the time my mother arrived, the police and a social worker were already at the school. I will never forget the look on my mother's face. It was the look of hurt, embarrassment, and anger. She took me straight to Methodist Hospital where the doctor performed a Rape Kit. After my mother, the doctor, and the police questioned me. My mother was taken into a room. I was left alone with the police. I was ten years old and terrified. To make matters worse, they kept asking me the same questions over and over again. I mean, how many times I had to tell them something I wasn't even supposed to be telling. I felt like I was killing myself over and over again, not to mention my mother seemed upset with me.

On the way home, my mother didn't say much of anything to me. I could tell she was mad, but I didn't know if it was with me or Bob. Once we got to the door, she pushed me inside. Enraged, she told me to go in the "fucking" room. I did as I was told crying the entire way. Romie was just looking at me but didn't say anything at all. As I sat in the bedroom, I could hear a lot of noise. It sounded like something was tearing and snapping. My mother stormed in the room and started beating me with the metal showercurtain rod. She was screaming ugly things. I tried to run. She closed the door. Romie tried to get her off of me. She hit him too. I managed to get under the bed, and my brother ran out the room. Relentless, she turned the rod the long way and continued to beat me under the bed. After she was done, I laid in a fetal position under the bed for the rest of the evening. Later that night, she came in the room and moved the bed, picked me up and placed me in the bed with her. She held me. She said she was sorry and wouldn't hit me anymore. My brother didn't come home that night.

A couple of days later Bob came over. I was so scared. My mother didn't allow him inside, but they had words in the front yard. I saw him hand her a lot of cash. She asked, "What the hell am I supposed to do with it?" She threw it all over the front yard. Bob left. I can't really say I saw too much of him after that. Later that week, my mother dressed me up in her clothes and drove me around to her friends' houses. She said since I wanted to be a girl she was going to introduce me as one. We saw a man. She said, "Hey, this is my little daughter Roberta." I remember him saying, "Come on Baby Girl. Don't do that to that boy." She asked him, "Why not? If he wants to act like a bitch, then I am going to treat him like a bitch." I was embarrassed to say the least. I didn't ask for Bob to touch me! I didn't want to do those things with him. It was like my mother didn't believe me. It was like she thought I wanted that man. After that day, I communicated with her only through letters. I would leave the letters where she could find them or hand them to her directly. I didn't have much to say. Plus, I was too afraid to talk to her.

CHAPTER SEVEN

CHILDHOOD DAYS

Some say that people are not born gay. They believe it is a learned behavior. For me, that would be false. I was born gay. Every child is born with a vision. It's up to the parent or the guardian to cultivate that vision, or it will be lost forever.

Growing up in DuSable Arms seemed normal to me simply because it was all I knew. Aunt Teresa's daughter, Latoya, was my life. We are eight months apart. She was my only girl cousin that lived in the projects and the only cousin around there I felt I could talk to. I wanted to be just like her in more ways than one. Latoya and I would make mud pies together while the other boys would play football or wrestle. I did not like to get dirty. I was a very clean kid.

I loved playing house with the other girls in the projects. If I wasn't the mother, I usually got upset. If Latoya was playing the mother, then I played the role as "the sister" and vice versa. She would ride her bike down the street, and I would follow behind her. I would walk my bike because I didn't know how to ride. No one cared to teach me. She shared her Barbie dolls with me. We would dress them up and do their hair. When Aunt Teresa moved to Colorado with her husband and Latoya, I was devastated. Latoya was gone. She left me behind with all my boy cousins.

******

I was six years old when my mom followed Aunt Teresa to Colorado. She left Romie and me behind with my dad, Robert. We stayed down the street from my dad's mom, Grandma Minnie. On days spent alone, I would go in the basement and play dress-up in some of the clothes my mother left behind. I loved her black high heels with the peep-toe. They fit on my feet perfectly. One day Romie caught me playing in the clothes and proceeded to beat me bloody. One hard swing to my left eye, and he busted it. Blood was everywhere. He didn't care. He kept hitting me and repeated, "I'm not having a faggot for a little brother. Fuck that!" Our relationship grew worse and worse. It was like he had taken my mother's place. He seemed to hate me so much.

A couple of months later, my mother moved Romie and I to Minnesota with her second husband, Gerald. Most of the family was moving there, so I was happy. Best of all, Latoya was there. We lived at 1909 Park Ave. It was nicer than Gary, but it was nothing special. We had a two-bedroom apartment on the first floor of a small brown brick building. Our couch was checkered green, and white. Romie and I slept on foldaway beds. We didn't have much of anything. There were times my mother would throw some crazy concoction together for Romie and me to eat, like Ramen Noodles with cheese whiz and bacon bits. She couldn't cook but she tried, ghetto food is what I called it. It's a bunch of nothing that tastes like something. They never sat at the table with us. She and Gerald would be sitting in the opposite room while we ate. When I asked Romie why they didn't eat with us, he'd dismiss me and tell me to mind my business. I rarely saw my mother eat and finally understood it was because we never had enough food for the four of us.

Minnesota wasn't what I thought it was going to be. I hardly got to see Latoya. When the family was together, Uncle Kenny was usually holding me in a room verbally abusing me and making Romie and I fight. Uncle Kenny would say things like, "You going to be a little girl! You evil! You ain't going to be nothing." Basically, Uncle Kenny said all the things no child wants or needs to hear. I don't believe I was ever really told I love you, as a child. Nor do I recall anyone trying to show or teach me anything.

Things weren't working out for mother and Gerald in Minnesota. Not long after moving there, we moved back to DuSable Arms Apartments in Gary. Gerald was the first man I saw hit my mother. Like any child, I jumped in and tried to help my mother. Gerald ended up hitting me once and busted my lip. I couldn't understand why my mother married him. He was no help. He actually brought her down. I know because I walked in the bedroom and witnessed them snorting cocaine.

When she finally decided to leave him, he came to the house while we were all sleep and tried to start a fire in the kitchen to burn the house down. My mother woke up when she heard the noise and grabbed her .357 Magnum and shot at Gerald. That's what woke Romie and me. There was so much smoke. That old gun was loud and smoking. She shot again, and missed of course. She was lucky not to shoot herself because the gun backfired. Gerald ran out the house, and we had no further problems from him.

There was really no time when my mother was "manless." It seemed, right after her relationship with Gerald ended, my mother brought Bob home. That ended after the molestation. Then she got a best friend, Pete. He was tall, skinny, and dark skinned. He wore a low haircut and appeared very well put together. He drove a blue or black Cougar and would come over sometimes. I would catch him staring at me awkwardly, and it made me slightly nervous. But he was a lot less creepy. I was now 10 and knew the differences. I did not want another Bob around. Their relationship was strictly platonic to the best of my knowledge.

******

I actually stayed more outside my mother's house than in it. I started floating between my dad's, my Grandma's house, and my mother's sister, Sylvia's house around 10 years old. I started to build a bond with Aunt Sylvia's son, Troy. He was two years younger. We were so different. He had love you could see.

Troy did boy stuff like wrestling, playing football, climbing trees, and jumping off things. He had bunk beds, and we would build castles on them. We threw the covers from the top of the bed and let them fall to the floor. We would pick a ruler and play like we were warriors; it was fun. Troy had so many toys. The thing that kept us sane was a Nintendo game system. We fought together in the neighborhood. He and I had the relationship I wanted with my brother. I envied Troy at times. He was my Grandma Hazel's favorite grandchild, and he got to go everywhere. They even took him to "Disney World", and I wasn't invited. My aunt Sylvia was amazing. Their relationship was beautiful. I wanted to be as close to my mother as he was. I wanted my family to love me the way they loved him. I always thought that my grandmother Hazel hated me. She used to call me dumb and would hit me, too. I felt like almost everyone with my mother's blood was violent. I even felt like some of them hated me.

I was in fourth grade when Grandma Hazel came to get me from school. It was record day, and I received five D's. My teacher explained to my grandmother how I was extremely playful, and I talked and sang constantly. She called me a stupid faggot and said I wasn't going to be a damn thing in this life. Another time we were in the kitchen. She slapped me, and said, "Get out of here! There ain't nothing but grown folks in here!" I must have taken my time trying to exit the room because she smacked me upside my head so hard I stumbled forward. The people in the kitchen just looked as if they were waiting for me to say something. I ran out the kitchen crying and holding my face. The thing that bothered me most about my Grandma Hazel, and a lot of my family, was neither she nor the others showed me any type of affection. It wasn't like they didn't know how because I saw everyone else get affection. I couldn't figure out why no one loved me like that. I wasn't alone though. Aunt Sylvia and Theresa had my back, as well as my dad. The one that showed me the most love was my Grandma Minnie. She was truly my world.

******

Yeah, my dad's mother, Grandma Minnie, was essential in my developmental stage. My mom would stay gone for days and not return, so I was always hungry. I called Grandma Minnie and told her that my brother and I were hungry and hadn't eaten. She came and took us to her house. I'll never forget what she said while we were cooking. "Give a man a fish, and you feed him for a day. Teach a man to fish, and you feed him for a lifetime." That's when she taught me to cook. Grandma Minnie was from the South and prepared everything from scratch, from the biscuits to the collard greens. I was happy someone was teaching me something—something beneficial to my well-being. There was hardly ever food in the house, but I made do with what was there.

Grandma Minnie owned Ule's Barbershop on Broadway with my grandfather. They owned a home on 19th Ave, a very nice area. They owned many cars and acres of land. Sometimes it seemed like I lived two separate lives. On one hand, I was in a housing project with nothing—not even food. On the other hand, I was in a mansion, as far as I was concerned, surrounded by toys. I had clothes at my grandmother's and was never hungry. I would have play dates with Michial, Grandma Minnie's bestfriend's grandson. I spent the night on weekends, and every Sunday, with Michial. I would get to go along with our grandmother to breakfast, the grocery store, and flea markets before going home to cook Sunday's dinner.

My grandmother was a big woman, about 250 pounds. One Sunday, in the Bob Evans' parking lot, she was getting out of the car and mistakenly hit the car next to hers. This old white man was coming out of the restaurant.

He let us know it was his car when he shouted, "You big fat nigger, hit my damn car." Before he could get another word out, Grandma Minnie put her hand in her purse and pulled out a small, chrome gun. "Call me another nigger!" She said with a hard stern voice. The man didn't. We went in and had breakfast. At the table, and again in a very stern voice, she said to me, "Don't take any shit from no one."

I was at Grandma Minnie's almost every weekend. The atmosphere was so relaxing and warm. Uncle Shawn, Grandma Minnie's grandson, was a big support as well. He was a year older than my brother and treated me like one instead of a nephew. His mother was raped, murdered and mutilated when he was six months old. Grandma Minnie adopted him so that he wouldn't have to spend his life in foster care. She raised him and sent him to college. You could tell he had different experiences because he was so well-versed and positive. I loved being around him.

My mother and I were leaving Town & Country Grocery Store and heard the most shocking news over the radio. The owner of Ule's Barbershop had just been taken into custody for the murder of two Tennessee State Troopers. My mother raced to my grand-mother's house where we were met by news cameras and reporters. Grandma Minnie was a wreck. I'll never be able to forget the look of hurt and shame on her face. Apparently, my grandfather shot and killed two state troopers on the highway. The police weren't sure why. He was not under arrest and was, in fact, assumed to be in duress in a ditch on the side of the road. The troopers came to aid him, and he shot them. He was 82 years old, with a record that dated back to the 1920's. Now he would die in jail.

The relationship between my mother and I was still shaky, extremely unhealthy, and volatile. With all that Grandma Minnie was now going through, I wasn't going to her house as often. When I was 12 years old, Aunt Sylvia said I could stay with her and my cousin Troy permanently. She took the responsibility for taking care of me. I credit her with saving my life. If I would have stayed, who knows what my mother would have done to me. I used to get beat so unmercifully, I could have been killed during any of her beatings. Before long, my little cousin Hazel was born, and I helped Aunt Sylvia take care her. I knew she needed the extra help. I was willing to give her help if it allowed me to stay with her. The way that she treated her children, and everyone else's children, really made me want to be raised by her. I knew in my heart and soul I was safe at all times. I wished and prayed on a daily basis that she would've adopted me.

******

I always wanted nice things and understood that hard work is normally how people got money. So I began to sell cupcakes and lemonade with the help of my aunt. Cupcake and lemonade combo sold for one dollar. I was doing well for myself. The neighborhood drug dealer, Boonie, usually bought all the cupcakes for more than they were worth and told me to give them to the kids in the neighborhood. I loved that because I didn't have to sit outside all day. If the kids really liked them, and they did, they would come and buy their own. It was how I was going to "come up."

I kept all my money in a piggy bank. I almost lost my mind the day I walked into my room and discovered it was empty. It couldn't have been anyone other than Romie. He would definitely steal from me. I confronted him in front of his friends. He didn't like that. I could see the evil that I had seen many times before in his eyes. I ran to Aunt Sylvia's house in fear that he was going to beat me up. I knew as long as I stayed in front of her I was safe. Later that evening, while Aunt Sylvia and I were watching TV, Romie walked in and punched me in the chest so hard it knocked the wind out me. I fell to the floor. My Aunt Sylvia went off on him, grabbed him up and asked was he crazy? He just looked at her, yanked his arm free and left. When I got my wind back, I told her I was going to get him back!

That evening I cooked us a nice dinner with macaroni and cheese, steak, and vegetables. I barely cooked the meat because I was inviting Romie. I wanted to serve him raw food for punching me. I had a skillet and a book out with my empty piggy bank when he came in to eat. He sat there eating his food. When he was almost done, I hit him in the head with the skillet and ran behind my aunt.

She would not allow him to hit me back. Thank God because he probably would have killed me. I cursed him out and told him I did that because he took the money I was saving. I told him the food was undercooked, and I hoped he got really sick for stealing from me. It was soon after that, that he stopped torturing me.

Living with Aunt Sylvia was amazing. She gave me life. She was caring, supportive, and uplifting. She told me I was smart and I could do anything that I wanted. I felt like she was a sister sometimes because we would sing to each other, and we laughed a lot. My aunt was a huge Michael Jackson fan and I was a huge *En Vogue* fan. I would sing to her. She would smile and clap, and say, "You go boy!" When she learned how to drive, she took me everywhere with her.

Aunt Sylvia stopped Romie from beating me so many times. When my brother would be literally torturing me, my aunt would come from next door because I would scream. She would save my life. I considered her my guardian angel. Romie would beat me until I bled. He figured he could beat me straight—always repeating he was not going to have a faggot little brother. Aunt Sylvia was always there. If anybody mistreated me, or even tried to mistreat me and she was around, she stepped in, no matter who they were.

******

I had so much pinned up frustration I began to beat my little cousin Troy and the kids in the neighborhood. Everything bothered me. I was a victim in so many ways and didn't know how to handle what was happening in my life. Almost every day I had a fight with someone new. If anyone said anything smart to me or to Troy, I would beat them up. Then at night while we would be at home, I would beat Troy for not fighting the kids in the neighborhood as well. I taught him that if I fight anyone, he was supposed to fight them too. That's exactly how it went going forward. Everyone knew if they fight me, they were going to be fighting Troy and vice versa. Aunt Sylvia could see the changes in me and didn't like them. Suddenly, I felt disconnected from her and stopped talking to her about things because I felt like no one really understood.

CHAPTER EIGHT

THE STAY WITH DAD

When I was twelve and going into the seventh grade, my mother married her new husband Tony. They lived in Aetna, Indiana, so I had to transfer to Kennedy King Middle School where I knew no one. It was the first day of class. I was wearing an old, tight, black tee-shirt, Romie's too big black pants and his old blue K-Swiss sneakers. It took two pairs of socks and stuffing them with tissue to make them fit. My mother drove me halfway to the school and told me to get out and to walk the rest of the way. I had no clue where I was but started walking anyway. I walked in circles for an hour trying to find this school. I sat on the curb and started crying. This lady asked what was wrong. I told her, and she was nice enough to give me a ride to the school.

I had wished something would happen, so I didn't have to go back home. The entire day I tried to think of a way not to go back home, but no luck. Between my mother and brother, going home was tough. With Aunt Sylvia on the other side of town, I had no escape. I caught the bus home and learned where the bus stop was from a couple of boys, so I wouldn't encounter the same problems from today the next day.

Two weeks into classes and I still didn't care for my new school or new environment. My mother was still crazy. My brother was selling drugs.

The new husband, well, he was my mother's husband. One September evening in 1991, while watching *Different Strokes* on TV, I was told that Grandma Minnie had a heart attack and was in the hospital. By the time we arrived, she had already passed. At this point in my life, I had no concept of death and dying. The impact of her death would not hit me until many years later. She was one of the few lights in my life. Now she was gone. I didn't know what I was going to do.

My dad knew my situation wasn't the best and said now that he had the entire house I could come live with him. I didn't even have to think about it. My father was nothing but good to me and so was his family. I wanted to be around that love, and soon. I was ready to move, my mother and brother were ashamed of me and the physical abuse had gone on for years. I knew that this wasn't the life for me and when I saw a way out, I took it.

Grandma Minnie's funeral and repast were held on September 12, 1991. My father came and got me and my stuff, and I was officially living with him. I had to transfer to Beckman Middle School. I didn't think I was going to like this school. I only knew a few of the kids there. Living with my father was an experience. At one point, we had everything, and then we had nothing. He sold the barbershop, land, trucks and everything else that held value, other than the house and the car. He split the profit with Uncle Shawn right away, and there was cash in the house. I had so many toys, games, shoes, clothes and jackets. I loved the new attention and things.

Even though my mother was still married to Tony, she started coming around my dad more. He had money now. That's all she cared about. She didn't stay around long. When her divorce from Tony was final, she ran off with a woman, Vicky. The entire situation was crazy and confusing to me. I had been beaten for years because I was gay, and here she was dating and having relations with a woman. It seemed all my mother cared about was what she could get from someone. Vicky had her own house in Glen Park. She was a registered nurse at the hospital, and she had a car.

By Spring 1992, I realized my dad was nice and caring, but his priorities weren't straight. He was a part of a bike gang called "Sin City Disciples" in Gary. He definitely provided financially but was not a good role model or teacher. He had his life and was always in and out with his friends. I wasn't being beaten anymore, but I still wasn't happy. I was always alone. I hated it. All the money and things couldn't get me the relationship I wanted, and soon the money was gone. He spent it and gave it all away.

I'm not sure if it was a sense of neglect or not, but after being with him for an entire school year, ALONE, my father came home and thought it would be nice to raise all his kids together. So Romie moved in, and we went to Chicago to get my sister LaShenia. She was given up at six months because my mother had gotten pregnant back-to-back, and Grandma Hazel said she had to choose between her and Romie. She couldn't keep both. I had seen LaShenia a few times, so I was excited. I was hoping she wasn't anything like my mother and Romie and instead would be the role model I needed.

There was a lot of unsupervised free time for Romie, LaShenia and me. Our cousins Lil Leon, Nikki, his sister, and Demetrius had come over for the weekend. We were all getting along without incident. Romie must have gotten bored and all of a sudden started calling me names. We went back and forth for a minute, and then he punched me in the face. LaShenia screamed and grabbed him. My eye started burning. I got one good punch in before Demetrius grabbed me. I was so mad that Romie hit me like that for nothing. I had a black eye and for no other reason than Romie feeling like it.

******

After that incident, my mom came over and accused LaShenia of sleeping with my dad and told her she had to go back to Chicago. She didn't even have a chance to get comfortable in school, and she was leaving. I guess you can say she came to visit for the summer. Either way, it was like *The Color Purple* watching my sister be ripped away from me by our own mother.

Romie went back to Aetna, Indiana to be around our cousins and his friends and to sell drugs. It was working out for him too. Whenever I saw him, he was fly, rocking whatever was the latest. Every now and again, he would even put a little money in my pocket.

Once LaShenia was gone, I really started to act out. I was gay in the eighth grade, and she was all I had. I created my own rule: if anyone said or looked at me funny, I would beat their ass. I ran into this girl Lela Lysol and had to eat my words. She wanted to be the most feared person in school. She started bullying me. It was more than I could handle. She was every bit of six feet tall and 200 pounds. I had heart, but at 5'5" and 110 pounds, I was nowhere near her size. I didn't even want that drama. Everyday she'd see me and call me a fag or a punk. She threw things at me and even spit in my face. My friend, Tiffanie, told me to stand up to her plenty of times, but I couldn't. I didn't know if it was more embarrassing to be verbally humiliated or physically humiliated. I went with the one that didn't hurt.

******

I had been home from school for a couple hours and my dad was nowhere around. I watched some TV and tried to find something to do. No one was outside because it was March and still a little chilly outside. The knock at the door startled me. I wasn't expecting anyone. It was my mother's friend Keona. She'd come to pick me up. She said that we had to go to the hospital right away. I had no idea what was going on. She was crying and speeding thru the lights and stop signs. When we arrived at the ER unit, the entire family was there. I heard my mother screaming and crying around the corner. Hearing her cry took something from my soul. I could feel her pain. I knew whatever it was, was bad. My aunt told me Romie had been shot. They didn't think he was going to make it. I felt bad. I was confused. He had caused me so much pain, but he was my brother. He had a six-month-old child. It was just too soon for him "to be gone permanently." They said Romie died three times during surgery. He was shot underneath his heart, and his spleen had to be removed. He turned out alright after that episode. I knew I wanted a better relationship with my brother. Life was way too unpredictable. I knew I had to cherish my relationships with my family.

******

At school things were all the same. My teachers complained about me. Some of the students hated me, and I was in hell. Lela bullied me so much; I was trying to find all kinds of ways to miss school. I stayed out of school for an entire week pretending to be sick. My mother came over and right away knew I wasn't sick. She asked me what was wrong, and I told her about my bully. She said I was going back to school, and the next time the girl said anything to me to beat the shit out of her, or she would beat the shit out of me.

That was all I needed to hear, I took nothing my mother said lightly. I was not trying to get beat. So I guess I would have to stand up to Lela. The next day I went to school. Lela called me a fag right before lunch. I went to my locker and got the two key locks I put in there that morning. I stood in front of my locker with the locks in my hand waiting for her to approach. She had everyone scared. I said this big bitch wasn't going to have me scared anymore. Before I knew it, she said fag, and I hit her before she could get out her next word. I tried to break every tooth in that bitch's mouth with that lock. There was so much rage and anger. I was trying to beat her bloody.

It wasn't going to be so easy though. Lela was massive. She picked me up and threw me into the lockers and bit me in my face. I started to hit her in the mouth with the lock. I was trying to hit her eyes or break her nose. She COULD NOT win! I wasn't going to get my ass whooped by her and then go home and deal with my mother. That made no sense! People tried to break us apart, but I wasn't having it. I went even harder. I had her hair locked in my hand and was beating her in the head with the lock. I couldn't even see.

I just knew where my target was and continued to aim. Once they finally got us apart, we both went to the office where our parents were called. Her father wanted me arrested, stating that I was a boy, and I had a weapon. My mother and father told the principal she had bullied me for too long, and I snapped. I was expelled from eighth grade, as she was able to stay and graduate. Completely unfair but she knew never to try me again.

A couple of months after Romie was shot, I was really alone. LaShenia, Romie, Uncle Kenny, Aunt Teresa, and her family were all in another state. Aunt Sylvia was no longer right next door. It was just my dad, and my mom, whom I now only saw about twice a month. Things started to get really crazy. My dad started doing drugs with his friends. He would have his friends over doing drugs. I would be in the basement with the boys. I started drinking and smoking weed and even having sex in the basement. My dad never knew, he was so caught in his drug addiction. It was like he couldn't see me when I was standing right in front of him. He couldn't even keep the house together anymore. It started with the lights, water, and gas all getting turned off, then late payments on property taxes. It was a mess, and it went on for a while. During the summers, I would go live with Aunt Sylvia or Janice, our neighbor, until he finally was able to get things back in order. I had many friends, but Janice's son and daughter were two of my close friends. They had the room available, so I really didn't mind staying with them when we were struggling.

I was 14, and I wanted some money of my own. High school was coming, and I really didn't want to continue to wear Romie's hand-me-downs. I didn't have anything else to do that summer. Tiffanie asked her dad if I could work at their store, Papa Adam's & Wordie's Stop & Shop, liquor store on one side and candy store on the other. He agreed. I was happy to have a job. I was getting paid under the table, which was fine because I was making money. Plus I got to see Tiffanie all the time, and it made our friendship much closer.

******

I was back on the block hanging with the boys. They started calling themselves "17th Ave Boys" because they started hanging out with the older boys from 17th Ave and drew up a lot of beef with the other crews. During the beginning of freshman year, "17th Ave" got into some beef with "2-1 Boys". There was a big fight, and "17th Ave" had beat up the "2-1 Boys" pretty bad. It was kid beef. We thought and figured they would take the ass whooping and keep it moving. Yes, there was still beef, but nothing another fight or two wouldn't fix. On October 20, 1993, I was home alone. Again, my dad was at work, and I was bored out of my mind. I called Michial to come over and keep me company. We smoked, got the munchies something serious and decided to walk to the store. It was raining outside, and it was nippy, but the munchies could not wait. I put on my pullover hoodie. We headed out the door. We were about five houses down the block when a car skidded and did a donut in the middle of 19th Ave. A boy hoped out the car looked directly at me and called "Taiwan". Taiwan was one of the "17th Ave Boys". We had the same jacket, and people used to get us mixed up all the time.

I thought he was from the neighborhood, so I started walking towards him. The rain was falling hard. The streetlight shining above him was so bright I couldn't make out his face. Squinting and focusing as hard I could to try and figure out who he was, I was completely unaware of what was really happening. Michial grabbed my arm and yelled, "Run!" We took off. We cut through a house and jumped the gate right before they started shooting. We were really running for our lives. We were jumping gate after gate, like hurdles, when I felt a deep burning sensation penetrate my back. It was immensely hot and snatched the wind from my body. I stumbled a little. Michial grabbed me and told me to keep running. We kept running.

We came across an abandoned house, and hid inside. The shooter walked right pass the house. He was looking around with his gun drawn. Talk about "a high blower"—my back was burning. I just wanted to get home.

A two-door red Ford Escort pulled up, and the boy jumped in, and we ran to Michial's house. His mother's car was there, but she was supposed to be at work. It was way pass his curfew, and he knew he would get in trouble, especially if he told her what had just happened. I didn't care about being in trouble. I wanted to get indoors and fast. When we got inside, his mother had a very puzzled look on her face. I begged her to take me to my aunt's house. She agreed. When I stood to exit the car, it felt like someone was holding a blowtorch to my back. I walked in Aunt Sylvia's dizzy and stumbling. I started to lift my jacket, and the expression on everyone's face gave it away. I fell to my knees and started crying. My older cousin "Stanky" ran by me outside and shouted, "They shot my little cousin about five times!" Aunt Sylvia was the only one calm. She placed a towel on my back, called 911 and got dressed.

I felt safe because my family was all around me so not to get blood all over Aunt Sylvia's things I waited outside for the ambulance. I also had a few calls to make, but I didn't want everyone listening. I called Danny from the "17th Ave Boys" to let them know that someone looking for Taiwan had just tried to kill me. I explained I got shot in the back, and the shooter was actually walking around looking for me. I told him to let Taiwan know he needed to watch his back because someone was looking for him.

The ambulance arrived 20 minutes later. I was so happy I wasn't *really* dying. Gary Police Department and local news reporters wanted to speak with me, and I obliged. After I told my story, my mom and dad came into the room.

My dad was crying and asking, "Who did this to you?"

Before I could answer, my mom jumped in his face and claimed, "This is your fault dumbass. You should have been home. You don't leave a 14-year old alone all night! I'm taking my fucking son back, and you will never see him again." Then she stormed out of the room and spoke with the reporters.

The bullet went in and out, so my recovery was quick. I was told if it had been a few inches to the left, the .9mm bullet would have hit my lung.

CHAPTER NINE

MY REAL DAD RETURNS

As soon as school was out, my mother made good on her promise. My dad's drug addiction had gotten worse. He couldn't keep the bills paid. My mother said she felt better when I was with her. I was very hesitant to move back with her. She was staying with Aunt Sylvia, so I thought I'd be okay. I was happy at my dad's even with the financial problems because he never took his frustrations out on me. My mother, on the other hand, had an on and off switch. One minute I was her baby and she loved me, next you would have thought I was some crack head in the street begging for money that she couldn't stand the sight of.

One night she asked me to get dressed, and we were going out. We weren't in the car long before we entered a familiar neighborhood. I saw Romie and LaShenia's grandparent's house and thought that was where we were going, but we pulled into another driveway. It was a big, side-by-side, tan house with a well-trimmed lawn—flowers, trees, yard ornaments, the works. It was a beautiful house, and it looked quite familiar. Walking to the door, my mother said nothing of where we were. So many things crossed my mind, I wondered if she was giving me away. Was she going to use me for trade? I never knew with her but this house was familiar and it actually made me feel safe.

An older couple came to the door wearing wide smiles. It was very confusing to say the least. Then I remembered I used to walk home from school this way. They would stop me and ask how I was doing. The lady gave me cookies. The old man would give me five and sometimes even ten dollars. Yes, these were very nice people. But why did my mother bring me here?

"Well, I told y'all I would bring over your grandson." What did she just say? These weren't her parents and my other grandmother just died, and my grandfather was in jail. Who were these people? The old lady smiled even harder. The old man's eyes filled with water. "You look just like your father!"

I just stood there with a sideways smile and a confused look on my face thinking, *what the hell is she talking about?* Before I could finish my thought, the old man grabbed me, gave me the warmest, tightest and most loving hug I'd ever felt. We all walked inside, I immediately noticed a picture of me and the old lady hugging. I thought, that could've been me. I couldn't recall when I would have taken it. The boy was dressed up in a suit and I surely did not own one. I must have been staring at the picture for a while because the old lady came behind me, placed her hand on my shoulder and asked, "You know who that is don't you?

I shook my head in confusion, "No, I thought it was me, but it is not."

She seemed sad at first and then giggled. "No child, that's me and your father when he was a little boy."

My heart started beating a million beats per second. I turned around, and my mother was talking with the old man.

"Mom, what is she talking about?" Then my mind started drifting, *I was in the ninth grade, four days shy of my 15th birthday, and she springs something like this on me? I had a dad. His name was Robert. I was named after him. He most definitely was my father. No, this could not be happening. She is playing a dirty trick. Wow, and got these nice old people to play with her. Terrible! Oh, my gosh! That would explain why they were so nice to me when...*

"ROBERT!" My mother's voice jolted me back to reality, "Pay attention! Yes, that is your father. These are your grandparents, Ma and Pa Holloway."

I didn't like the way I was feeling. I reached out my hand, slightly nervous and with an unexpected stutter replied, "Nice to meet you."

We sat and talked and ate a little. They showed me pictures and told me my father's name was Samuel, but he went by Pete. Pete, then I remembered the man's face. I met him a couple of years ago. I looked just like this man. There was no denying it. I was so confused. *"Why would they tell me this now? What was going to happen with Robert? Why do I have his name if he's not even my father?"* My head was spinning.

I left the house with a smile, but inside, I was so angry. I already had a father, which was all I kept thinking. He was someone who had always been there for me, cried for me, and even though he was a drug addict, he tried hard to take care of me. He never beat me or neglected me. I felt that my mom was doing this out of spite, and that just further upset me. Pete. Well, if Pete was my dad, then where the fuck had he been? That house was so nice. He even had nice clothes as a child, so that let me know they had some kind of money. Here I was wearing shoes two sizes too big and recycling the same four outfits; moving from house to house with no stability or guidance! Getting my ass beat at my mother's will! Living in the projects! I was going through hell, and I have a father who had better and didn't even acknowledge me? What the fuck?!

I was eating my nails down to my finger meat. I was asking and answering a million questions in my head before my mother finally said something.

"I met your father a long time ago. He and I were good friends. He was married, but I liked him a lot. One night we 'happened' and a few nights after that, but Pete was married. I don't know what I thought was going to happen. I told him I was pregnant. His response was that he was not leaving his wife. I was pregnant alone for the most part, but Robert wanted to be with me. Robert knew he was not your father. He was head over feet in love with me. Two months after you were born he asked to marry me. I was thinking, *another child with no father,* no I wasn't doing that. He told me he was going to raise you as his own, as long as your father had nothing to do with you. I was mad because he did not want me, so I agreed."

I stared at her in astonishment. She was so selfish. I could understand my father was married and not going to leave his wife but to make an agreement not to let him have a relationship with me was selfish. I didn't say anything. I just sat in the car patiently waiting to get home. How could I get far away from her? I was mad. No I wasn't. I was FUCKING PISSED!

******

My birthday had come and gone, and Christmas was on its way. I wasn't one of those holiday kids. I usually got underwear, socks, t-shirts and things like that. The weather was incredibly cold, so a bigger jacket would be nice, but if I got anything I was grateful. Snow was falling on a regular, so being outside wasn't a real option, and sitting at Aunt Sylvia's with everyone was driving me crazy. There just wasn't enough space.

It was the weekend and really cold outside. No one wanted to go anywhere. The entire house was home to Aunt Sylvia, Mother, Troy, baby Hazel and me. We were all sitting in the living room watching TV. An unexpected knock at the door threw everyone off. No one was expecting company, so no one moved to answer the door. I got up when the person knocked again. I opened the door and felt like I was looking into an aging mirror. It was the man in the picture, my father. There he stood. He was a tall, dark-skinned man with little eyes and full lips. He was slim and square in the face with a pudgy nose. It was so creepy. He looked just like me.

The cold swept pass me, and I realized I was staring at him with the door open. "Come in," I offered.

He reached out to shake my hand. "Thank you."

I really didn't want a handshake. I wanted a hug, but I shook his hand anyway. Aunt Sylvia, mother and my cousins stayed in the living room while we talked in the kitchen.

"How are you doing?"

I guess he couldn't think of anything else to say. In my mind I thought, *Can't you see? What the hell you think? It's like five of us in a two-bedroom apartment in the projects.* But I didn't want to scare him away. "I'm good."

"I'm sorry that I missed so much time and wasn't around to aid in raising you?"

Blank Stare

"I really did not want it to be like this."

Blank Stare

"I was married. I had a family. I know it's no excuse but sometimes..."

I just cut him off.

"It's okay. We can get to know one another now."

I wasn't interested in the sob story. I had my own. I was open to getting to know him. As much as I loved my dad Robert, he was on drugs and really was unable to do anything for me now. His house was like a drug hotel. Whenever I thought I wanted to go stay with him, I'd walk pass the house, and there'd be people in the front speed-balling. I wanted that real father figure in my life. If that's what he was proposing, I was willing to accept.

"It's not going to happen overnight. I don't know you. There's a lot to know about me, but I'm very willing if you are." He said that was fine. We hugged. He gave me $250, and told me he was going to be there from now on to make sure I was okay. I was smiling inside. I believed him.

CHAPTER TEN

I WAS GOING TO BE DIFFERENT

New Year and New Year's resolutions were some things I was not interested in. What was I going to vow to change just because it was 1994? NOTHING! I was still in the damn projects. Everything and everyone else was the same. Why should I change? I had been shot, I was gay, and I had an unstable home life affecting my grades. To top things off my mother was crazy and I had two fathers. What needed to change? I was going to be a product of my environment!

******

After Christmas, my mom moved back in with Vicky. I would have my own room again, so I was in complete compliance. Vicky lived further from school than Aunt Sylvia, and my mother had to pass her job to take me to school. It eventually became a problem. I wasn't with her a solid month before she really started complaining about the drive back and forth to school. She wanted me to transfer. I did not want to go to another school. I begged her not to transfer me. I was 14 and gay. Getting comfortable in another school would be hard. I already had friends and a half decent relationship with my teachers. The people at Roosevelt High School were comfortable with me. I was comfortable with them. I was not going to a new school and starting over. Transferring to Lew Wallace High School was asking for trouble. She didn't care. I ran up to my bedroom, crying, telling her I would have to fight because people would mess with me since I was gay.

She followed me up the stairs and stood in the doorway with her hands on her hips. "Well, then maybe you shouldn't be gay."

I turned around with tear filled eyes completely shocked. "How can you say that? You are living with a woman, and she is your girlfriend?"

She didn't like that response at all. "You don't need to worry about what I'm doing. I'm grown. Now get your skinny ass up, and let's fucking go. I'm not driving you to that school everyday. This is not an option!"

When I knew she was completely down the steps, I screamed, "You're going alone because I'm not coming if we're not going to Roosevelt." I must have forgotten who I was talking to.

"What the fuck did you say?" She started back up the steps.

I jumped off the bed and ran to close the door. I knew that wouldn't be enough because when she was mad she was a monster, so I pushed the bed against the door to prevent her from getting in.

She screamed, "You must have really lost it, Robert! You better open my fucking door you faggot!"

I was full of courage behind the door. "If I'm a fag then you're a dike!"

That must have really pissed her off because She started beating on the door even harder. I figured it was best if I opened it. She rushed in and began to hit me. I was so tired of the abuse. I put my hands in her face and pushed her off of me. She bit her lip and when she saw the blood, she screamed, "Oh yeah, I got the perfect place for you. Your faggot ass got heart now. See how much heart you have in jail. Think you can put your hands on me you little bitch!"

Talk about crazy. She was so mad I hit her back she wanted to send me to jail. All the years of abuse and bullshit, I didn't know how to feel.

She walked out the room, and I closed the door behind her. I could hear her on the phone crying and playing the victim. I didn't think she was really calling the police. I don't know why I doubted her. They came to the house in two squad cars. I could hear them coming up the stairs lead by a bunch of lies. She told them I was violent and needed to go to jail. I had no desire to go to jail. I tried to tell them she was lying and, in fact, jumped on me. I begged them to look at my face. They didn't acknowledge my plea or ask me any questions. I was put straight into handcuffs, and into the back of the squad car I went. I couldn't believe she really had me arrested!

They only held me for a couple of hours. My mother didn't want to press charges. She just wanted to prove a point. She was so childish. The craziest part was I never transferred after all of that. I was still attending Roosevelt. Even though I was happy I didn't have to transfer, I still wasn't in love with school. It was a rough place. People used to talk about my clothes and call me names. I had the boys from the block, but they weren't really in attendance so I was alone most times.

******

By April, I was back living at Aunt Sylvia's house. My mother and Vicky were arguing back and forth which bothered me. Aunt Sylvia lived close to my school, so I decided it would be better if I stayed there. I'd become sexually active, and started to enjoy it.

Michial was just like me, and we shared everything. This particular evening we covered a lot of information.

The phone rang. "Hey bitch!!!"

"Hey Boo!!!" I loved Michial.

"Bitch, your side was live yesterday."

They opened the fire hydrant in the projects and all the boys in the hood were shirtless in the water.

"I know, I could hardly contain myself, did you see all those bodies?"

"You know I did! Yes Lord, you know I did! I would make them niggas scream! Especially that really caramel candy looking nigga! What's his name again?"

Michial was talking about "Double G." He was fine as hell.

"Well, just because you're interested, I should let you know, that's 'Double G', and I had sex with him. Him and 'Coop.'"

Michial was so shocked, "Bitch you nasty! And you just telling me? I can't believe you. They best friends bitch! And you are just telling me? I'm mad at you! How was it?"

I burst into laughter. All Michial wanted to know was what the dick was like so I told him. "Well, first bitch, I didn't do them at the same time. I don't think I'm ready for that." We laughed. "Coop' got a mean bow leg, and it's so sexy. I just had to see what he was working with, plus he ain't gay like us. Humph, so he pays me. You know I need my own money. He wants me to keep it a secret, so he hit me off. I hit him off, and we keep moving."

Michial replied sarcastically. "So you out here fucking for them dollars, huh? Oh well girl! Do what you have to. Now what about 'Double G'?"

It was true. I did need the money, so I didn't care. My mother did it. Why couldn't I?

"I only sucked that nigga's dick. Oh, and he got a nice..."

"Hang up my phone!" I was totally shocked but not afraid. I just hung up. Aunt Sylvia had been listening in the entire time. She heard everything I said. I didn't know how it was going to end. She came into the room with a nasty tone. "So you are gay?"

She had already heard the truth, so there was no sense in lying, "Yes!" I confirmed with a very stern tone and look.

I don't think she knew any other way to respond. "Don't you ever put your lips on my baby again! Sucking dick, and kissing my baby, how disgusting!"

I was so offended. Hazel was no more than two years old. I would never kiss her, as soon as I finished doing something like that. I knew this was going to become an ordeal when I heard the phone dialing. Aunt Sylvia called my mother and within the hour half of the family knew I was actively gay. Family in Minnesota I hadn't seen or spoken to, family in Indiana that didn't even bother with me, everyone, knew. It didn't matter if I was ready or not. It was now my reality.

******

On April 23rd, 1994, my mother picked me up and said we were going for a ride. She was very calm. She seemed okay. She hadn't said much to me directly about what Aunt Sylvia overheard. I figured it was because she was living with a woman, so she understood I was just like her.

While we were driving down Virginia Street, she told me my life was going to be very hard if I chose to be gay. I was gay. I didn't care about what other people thought, as long as my family was behind me and supportive. I would be okay. We pulled up to the 13th Ave Police Precinct. I didn't know why we were there. I followed her inside where she met an officer. They escorted me into a room and walked away together. I don't know what they talked about. He came back into the room without my mother. He told me to stand up, and I was under arrest. He took me into a cell. I sat in a holding cell for a couple of hours, then was put in a squad car and taken to Lake County Juvenile Detention Center in Crown Point.

I cried the entire ride. All I could think about was I am going to jail for being gay? I had to man up. I couldn't go into this place looking weak. I was a fighter. I had a really bad mouth. I could handle this.

My mom would come visit me at times. Nothing was different. Everything was my fault. I might as well get used to the environment I was in because that's where I was going to be if I was gay. I hated her visits. I really did. She was degrading, demeaning, and unsupportive. She knew I was a ward of the state. If she said I had done anything wrong, they would put me back in a detention center. I hated her. To make matters worse, I had to be stripped searched to go back to the cells.

I was there for one month. That experience fucked me up! I didn't want to be gay anymore, but that's who I was. I liked boys and not girls. I couldn't change that. Upon my release, I was ordered to take counseling along and with my mother. We went three to four times a week. I thought it was going to be a way for me to openly express myself and figure out a plan moving forward.

To start, the sessions were slow. I was scared to say anything to the counselor that would make my mother look bad because I wasn't trying to have the drama later. My mother tried to force Romie to go, but he didn't have much to say I assumed. The counselor asked a few questions, and my mother broke down crying and sobbing. I couldn't stand to see my mother hurt. She never showed a lot of weak emotions, so when she cried, it cut deep. She was still my mother, and I loved her. I never wanted to see my mother in pain regardless of how much she had caused me.

The longer we were there, the more personal the questions and the deeper the conversations got. She asked me if I would meet with her alone, and I agreed. In that room, for the first time, I was asked, in a million different ways, had I ever been touched. I wasn't sure how to respond. NO!

I had not ever been "touched." Then she asked if I was gay and why I was. The questions offended me. If I was gay, why did she care? I had no idea what all the "touching" questions were about. Was she trying to set me up? Get me to tell her certain things so she could tell my mother? I denied everything. I didn't say I was gay, having sex, smoking weed or anything because I did not trust her. Romie stopped going to the sessions completely. I wasn't too fond of them either.

******

When I got back to school everyone seemed to know my business and the teasing and bulling really poured in. Lester, Tiffanie and Michial had my back. They lived on the opposite side of the school, so they couldn't be with me all the time.

There were these two girls in my African American Studies class who must've been best friends. I always saw them together, I wanted that. A friend to always have. Michial was my friend, but we have been a little distant since the "Double G" conversation. He lived the opposite way so we couldn't walk together. The walk home was long and lonely. A best friend would've made the walk better and the bullying better, it would make everything better.

A lot of kids walked the same route home because many of them lived in the projects. I usually walked by myself and didn't pay much attention to the people around me.

"Hey Fag!" "Aye, Fag boy!"

"Faggot! I know you hear us talking to you!"

There were three of them and they were all screaming at me. I was tired of fighting. Why couldn't I just be me? I wasn't bothering anyone. Damn!

Someone hurled a rock right by my head and then another. I was trying not to turn around because I didn't want to fight. I just wanted to go home. "Leave that boy alone! He hasn't done anything to y'all fools."

I immediately turned around to see who was talking. My heart was smiling. This girl just stood up for me, no one had ever done that.

"His gayness is affecting the quality of my air."

"He can't handle his trouble. He shouldn't be gay, punk ass faggot!"

I turned around and looked at all of them.

"Well come beat this fag's ass bitch!" I replied.

They came rushing towards me. My heart was beating fast, but I wasn't scared. One girl stood in front of me while the other stood by my side. "If y'all fight him, y'all fighting us!"

The boys backed away while calling me names.

I was so shocked and happy. I wanted to cry but I couldn't look like a punk so I held back my tears. They really stood up for me. They started their introductions: Angela was a gorgeous, chocolate, brown girl with pretty eyes, hair done, thick hips and busty. Keisha was copper, and she shinned like a new penny. She had the prettiest light brown eyes and a really nice shape but she looked pregnant. I knew exactly who they were, and I was happy they liked me.

Ninth grade was coming to an end, and I was ecstatic. It was a hard year, both privately and publicly. I had been shot. Found out I had two daddies and arrested twice for bullshit! My attire was horrible. I was gay, and everyone knew it. Just when I thought all was well, Preston Sables, someone who had been taunting me off and on throughout my freshman year, was at it again. He taunted me so much by saying the nastiest things. He was straight up mean. It bothered me so badly. The sad thing was it bothered me not because of what he was saying, but because he was really cute. He had a stocky build with a caramel complexion, pretty eyes, nice lips, and my height. The way he acted was so completely unnecessary. Despite the fact that I was attracted to him, I still couldn't allow him to keep up the nonsense.

It was the word "faggot" really. I just didn't like it. I wasn't a faggot. I was a gay male. Preston had his chances. He didn't rectify his situation, so I did it for him. He was calling me a faggot when I busted him in the face. I picked up the school desk and tossed it. Once he was on the ground I blacked out. I hear it was a big mess though. His face was bloody, and his lip was busted. No more problems out of Preston. I was expelled behind the fight, but I didn't care. Sometimes we just have to stand up for ourselves. My mother didn't feel any remorse about my expulsion either. We knew the process for lifting an expulsion. We decided I would go to summer school to make up the credits.

******

West Side High was something else. I was happy I didn't attend here during the normal school year. All the schools in Gary met here for summer classes. That meant a lot of people from different hoods with different beefs would be in the same environment. Three days in and I heard someone call my name. It was the bitch I whooped on in eighth grade, Lela Lysol. How did this happen? Here we go again. I wasn't nervous. In fact, I was hoping she would get out of line because I would have an opportunity to beat her ass again.

She ran up, "Hey, how you doing?"

I was completely shocked. "Hey, I'm good."

There was no reason for me to stick around. I wasn't interested in conversing with her. I was here for a reason and didn't need any negative people around me.

******

I noticed him in what must have been the first week of my sophomore year. We were at a sock-hop in the gym during lunch hour. He was very gay, extremely flamboyant in fact. I mean he was red bone, 6'3", 180 pounds, with a full mustache and beard. He had a deep-ass voice. Rocking a "Bob." You couldn't help but notice him, and everyone did. People were all around him while he danced. I was in idol love. He was comfortable being himself. No one was fighting him or calling him a fag. I wanted to be just like him. I just wanted to have fun. All the fighting and drama was draining. I thought if I looked and acted like him, I wouldn't have to fight or worry about people talking about me. So I introduced myself to him.

He was extremely cool. His name was Moon, and he was a senior. He stayed in Delaney Projects, across the street from the school. He said it was good for business. He did hair, and no one had a problem walking there after school. He took me under his wing and became my role model. I felt very comfortable with my new friends. They never judged my appearance or behavior. I loved them for that. My friend from seventh grade, Lester, was Moon's cousin. He was always around. Then Angela and Michial got to know him. I was so excited that my friend circle was tight. I was growing a box fade, like "Kid" from "Kid-n-Play" used to sport, so my hair was a nice length. It wasn't at all feminine. That's what I was going for, so Moon did me up. He didn't charge me. He knew I was broke, but he still worked it out and laid my hair down so smoothly. It was an asymmetrical "Bob", and it was fierce! Tenth grade was panning out fine. I was in love with myself and my friends. Once Moon put the final touches on me, I was a force to be reckoned with.

My mother snapped the first time she saw my perm. I didn't expect anything else. She went into her degrading bag and called me all kinds of fags. "So what you think you look good now? You a girl? Got a perm and now you a real woman, huh?"

I didn't reply. I could have cared less about what she thought. She never had anything positive to say and had never embraced me. Eventually, I just stopped caring. She was mad I was ignoring her. I still didn't care. I just let her talk.

＊＊＊＊＊＊

By spring I was my own person. My friends had my back, and I would dare somebody to front. I was not trying to fight everyday and act up. I was interested in looking nice, having fun and boys. I was in counseling with my mother for a year and with no progress. I hated going to the sessions. She always wanted to make it like she was the ultimate victim. I was learning how to deal with her.

Over a year had passed since I had seen my father, and he had given me the $250, and said he was going to be around from that day forth. So when he came to the door late April 1995, I could have cared less. I still had my hair wrapped in my silk scarf. I was walking around in my aunt's fuzzy slippers and felt like my mother should entertain him. I was fine without knowing him. He was the one who introduced himself to me and still acted as if I didn't exist. I really had nothing to say. He was being a great dad somewhere else, while his only biological child was in a two bedroom, five people deep. He was a stranger to me. No clout, no authority—he was just a man. So when my mom tried to embarrass me and told me to take off my scarf and let him see my hair, I did so with no hesitation. His response was what it should have been, quiet. Who was he to say anything, anyway? I wasn't falling for his tricks again. I wasn't the same naive 14-year-old. I was 16. If he wanted a relationship with me, he had a lot of proving and respect-gaining to do.

That summer was long and boring. Moon graduated and hung with his drag queen friends, more and more and my mother was becoming the most annoying woman in the world. She just would not stop talking. How long everything be wrong? I just couldn't understand it. I was 16 and sharing a couch, not even a bedroom. I was completely annoyed. My dad, Robert, was doing really bad. I felt for him. He was completely drugged out and had lost Grandma Minnie's house. I had no idea where he was staying, but I wished him the best. I tried to keep a smile. Counseling was becoming a pain. I was so ready for it to be over. My mother and I were constantly at it, so why was I spending another summer in this room? That psycho even tried to make me take three, sometimes four, showers a day, saying I smelled of a homosexual. I wanted school to start. Junior year meant only a year before I could move away from this drama.

CHAPTER ELEVEN

AGAINST THE GRAIN

The plan for junior year was to be home as little as possible. My school had a huge selection of after school programs. I just had to find the ones for me. Espirit Modeling Troop was a competition based modeling program. They held fashion shows at the school and other locations. The entire school was eligible to try out. Modeling was fierce. I could be fierce! Plus it lasted three hours after school. PERFECT! Tryouts weren't until October. I had time to perfect my fierce. Everyone was supportive. The girls said I was an attention whore, and it would be great for me. Michial thought it was daring. It was. I was sick of having to hide myself. I could model just as well as any girl or straight male. I was going to do just that!

The day of Espirit tryouts I was pumped! The auditorium was packed. Moon was volunteering at the school as the model and drill choreographer. He really wanted me to make it. He styled my hair into high freeze (lifted finger waves for those that don't know) with a blue patch in the front. He helped me with all my points and turns. I WAS READY! Once I saw the first couple of people complete their tryouts, I was a little nervous. I made a statement. I wanted to make a bigger one. It was all or nothing. They showed us the walk. Called us up one by one, according to the number we had. They called my number, and I hit the stage hard. I looked all the judges directly in the face while walking straight towards them with high knees and a hard switch. I walked back. Hit the corners of the stage with the same energy. BAM!

I made my presence known. BAM! Here I am again. I worked it hard. There was no wonder they would choose me for the team. I WAS ECSTATIC!

I never anticipated that my mother was ever going to be happy with anything I did. When I told her I made the squad, her reaction was negative, repeat of times before. Things between us were getting worse by the day. She saw me trying to live outside of her evil; she hated it. I was getting bigger, so she wasn't hitting me anymore. Word play was her game of choice now—verbal abuse. I was a bitch, a little girl, a faggot, and a sissy and other words I would never repeat. She kept air fresheners throughout the house. At random she would come in whatever room I was in and spray the can half empty. I would literally choke. I really couldn't stand when she turned the radio really loud to wake me on days I didn't have to go to school. Or, she would keep it loud at night when I had to get up in the mornings. She was so draining.

We were practicing every day for our first show on November 17th, 1995. It was a big deal. There were flyers posted. Everyone was talking about being there. My nerves were running. The closer we got to the date, the more excited I got. My mother told me she wasn't coming. I told her that was fine. She didn't like my nonchalant attitude and tried to get me worked up anyway she could. I was sad our relationship was so hostile, but there was nothing I could do. I was still a ward of the state. That's why I kept going to counseling and tried to ignore my mother's ignorance. I didn't want to get in trouble. I had a court date November 14th for a routine meet with the judge. She just wanted to ensure I was behaving and not being a truant. My mother told the judge I was acting out and getting in trouble in school. She told lies on top of lies. The judge had me arrested. ARRESTED! I was three days shy of my big debut, and I was being arrested!

******

I thought this visit was going to be short. When I went into booking, I could have killed someone. Why did my mother hate me so much? Why would she do this to me? I knew then she didn't love me at all. How could she get away with this? I was like an orphan. She was the only person who took care of me. It was her or jail. Really, who was going to speak up for me? Pete was living his own life. Robert was strung out on heroin. They didn't know where I was. As far as I knew, they weren't even concerned. As far as I was concerned, the devil controlled my happiness at the tug of a string. He had just tugged it.

I was sick. I missed my first Espirit modeling show. But when I missed Thanksgiving, I cried. I was still in jail. Why wasn't anyone worried? The only person who came to visit was "Evilleana" (my mother). Every time she put me in jail, she came to visit to throw more dirt! She said it was my fault I was in jail. If I'd been more respectful, she wouldn't have to resort to these measures. I didn't care about anything she had to say. My hatred grew for her daily. When my birthday came and went, I almost flipped. I had no reason to be there. I wanted out!

This boy tried to calm me down. He told me all those things that didn't matter. I didn't want to be bothered, but he was cute, so I made an exception. His face was very familiar. If I didn't know him, I wanted to. Jonathan, an unexpected name, and he went to Roosevelt High School. That's when it clicked. He was on the modeling troop. He said he was here because his mom screamed assault. I laughed, said my mother did that once, but I didn't know why I was in there now. She was mad and decided to lie. I was missing school and my friends. I needed to get out. Jonathan became a great friend. He was gay as well, so we were able to talk about everything. Having him as a friend helped pass the time a little faster, and that was good.

Christmas and New Years came and went. I was steaming. Not because I was missing out on presents and things, but because I was just straight up missing life. I had had enough. By now I was 17, and I was still dealing with this sideways nonsense. I was in there two months before they let me go. I was released on January 14, 1996. I was so happy to get out of there.

Mother said if anyone asked, I was to tell them I had been in a mall fight and gotten arrested. She couldn't have people know the truth. The truth was that she had me in a detention center for two months because she had a hair up her ass. I stuck with the story, only so I wouldn't have to hear her mouth. I wasn't going to let her send me back to jail, not ever again, not for anything!

******

Getting back into the swing of school was not so difficult. I had good grades before I went to jail, and my teachers held them, and I went forward. It was like I hadn't even missed two months of school. The only thing people wanted to know was where I had been. I told them the detention center and what I did to go. I kept with the lie my mother told me and went about my business.

My mother's father passed on April 8th, 1996. I was very sad. He loved me unconditionally. He never judged me and always protected me and supported everything I did. I used to go visit him randomly. We would talk about everything. I was going to miss him so much. It seemed the entire family came for the funeral, and they were all staying with us. We had not been around each other like this in years. This was the first time everyone was around since I had become "officially" gay. Some of them were very standoffish and even talked about me while I was in the room, but didn't say a lot to me. Others were bold, and direct. I was a faggot. They didn't like it. Until I got my life right, they wanted nothing to do with me. I didn't care. Well, honestly, I did. What could I do? I was who I was, a gay male. I loved the same and cared the same, but apparently I was someone else. I just didn't bother with it. I was still on Espirit. I stayed after school and kept to myself and my friends. The last thing I wanted was to fight one of my cousins or argue with my aunts or uncles. They were there for a funeral, and then they were going back to Minnesota and wherever else. I paid them no mind.

NO PRACTICE! I loved Espirit, but sometimes I did not have the energy to stay after school. It was a nice day, and everyone was outside. Yes, I was happy there was no practice. Just like niggas from the projects, my entire family was outside. I even spotted Romie! It had been almost two and a half years since I last saw him. I was excited. Romie's sentiment was not the same. When we locked eyes, he charged at me like a wild beast screaming, "Faggot, you stupid, faggot, sissy ass, pussy bitch!" I didn't even have time to respond. He was on me! Everyone gathered around and watched him punch me dead center in the face. He had gotten big, but I wasn't that small anymore either. We were on the ground. I was swinging like a wild woman. I wasn't scared. I was actually really mad. This boy still hadn't grown up. He was repeating, "I told you I wasn't going to have no faggot as my little brother." REALLY!? If I had known being gay was going to be this hard for this long, I really would have tried girls. I was fighting my brother in the middle of the projects. Everyone was standing around watching, even my family. I wasn't the same Robert though. I wasn't going to sit there and allow him to attack me. I fought him just like everyone else. He wanted to act like a nigga in the street, so I fought him like a nigga in the street with no mercy. Finally, my friends stepped in. It felt like we had been fighting forever. When they were pulling us off the ground, there was an open shot. I kicked him in his mouth as hard as I could. I busted his lip wide open.

I was crying my eyes out. Even though I was crying, they were not tears of sadness. I was straight mad! Angela, Michial and Keisha were pulling me back. I kept screaming, "Let him go! Let his fuck ass go! I'm not afraid of that bitch!" Romie was shocked I stood up to him. My mother, being the Robert supporter she was, yelled for them to let both Romie and me go. Angela stood in front of me and said directly to my mother, if I was going to fight, she was going to be fighting with me. Keisha said the same thing. I just decided to leave. I didn't want my friends to fight my family because I knew that's exactly what it would have come to. My family was crazy. I didn't want them in that drama. We left and went to Angela's. It felt good knowing that there were people that had my back. I stayed at Angela's for the night. When I called home the next morning, Aunt Sylvia said Romie was gone, and it was okay for me to come home.

After the funeral, everyone went separate ways. I didn't want to be bothered with anyone and kept to myself and my friends. I finished the school year. All I could think about was next year I was going to be a senior. I could finally leave this GOD forsaken life.

******

My mother finally got her own place in the Color Doors Projects. It was an upgrade from DuSable Arms, but it was still the projects. I finally had my own room, and with senior year approaching, it couldn't have come at a better time. We were barely unpacked, when Romie called to tell mother his twin girls had arrived on July 10, 1996. I was happy for him. We hadn't spoken since the fight. I wasn't really interested in speaking to him. Mother, however, went straight to Minnesota to see her grandchildren. I stayed home alone. It was so relaxing. I called Keisha and Angela, and they stayed the weekend. We cleaned up and arranged things in the apartment. I felt like I had my own place for a minute. There was no drama for more than 72-hours. It wasn't normal, but it felt so good!

Everything was in order when Mother returned. The trip to Minnesota must have been just what she needed. She was smiling, glowing and extremely pleasant. We were getting along beautifully. All I could hope was for things to stay just like this.

******

I walked through the double doors beaming. It was the first day back to school. I was a senior. Making it this far meant a lot to me. Romie was a dropout. In six months I would be breaking the cycle. I had a fresh perm and a tight "Bob" I even added weave so it could swing just the way I wanted. The day went without incident. I loved it. I wasn't trying to fight, argue or defend myself. I'd been at this school for four years and everyone knew me. They knew I would fight whoever and whenever. So they finally just stopped bothering me. My focus was plain. I wanted to graduate! Once I was out, I would no longer be a ward of the state and would be free to live as I wanted. I had the same friends. They weren't going anywhere. Lester, Michial, Jonathan, and, when he wasn't running the streets, Moon. I had the best circle of friends, and I knew it. We were real with each other, had each other's backs, and no matter what, never fought! My Aunt Sylvia even warmed up to my lifestyle and allowed me to be around Hazel again. Hazel was my baby. I was there the first day she came home. I loved her so much, I was happy my aunt knew I was the same person inside and decided to accept me and support me regardless of my sexuality.

Senior year was magnificent. I liked a few boys. All of them were straight and had girlfriends. I didn't care. They were innocent crushes. Dennis Brewer and Andre Hazelton were seniors. John Williams was a junior. They were handsome and dressed nicely. I loved them hard on the inside. They all had girlfriends who eventually found out I was crushing on their boyfriends. Girls can't ever keep their mouths shut. That didn't stop me from liking them. I knew they were straight. It wasn't as if I was going to make any advances. Again, they were just crushes.

It may have been because John and his girl were younger that they thought it would be funny to toy with me. I played right along. They would laugh when they saw me. To piss them off, I would look directly at John and smile purposely just to give them something to talk about. They knew what the look meant. I wasn't subtle. I'd only been with "straight" guys anyway. I felt if I really wanted him I could've had him. Everyone else just wouldn't know. Niggas was like that. They would fuck a nigga and go back to their girl. They would "Keep it on the down-low. Nobody has to know", like the R. Kelly song. Neither John nor his girlfriend ever jumped stupid.

They knew I was crazy. I'd fight both of them and beat both of their asses. I didn't care.

Halloween fell on a Thursday and we were allowed to wear our costumes to school. I went as a woman, head to toe. At first it was just a thought. It was nothing that I was really going to actually do. Then I found a silver, sequenced, Daisy Duke jumper and knew I had to make a scene. It was my last year. What could it hurt? I walked into school in 6" silver stilettos with white fishnet stockings, my sequence jumper, a full B cup bra, lipstick and of course, my wrap. I learned how to tuck my penis, and I shaved off all my facial hair. I was a woman, indeed. They wanted to kick me out before the day had even begun. They said we could wear our costumes and didn't have any specific guidelines. I bet they would think about that the following year.

They were talking that day but by Monday, I was the talk of the school and all the other schools in Gary. Last period was interesting. Some girls and a few boys were saying negative things about me as if I couldn't hear them. I was serious about the no fighting thing however I had to say something, so I simply stood up and said, "What y'all mad cause I look better then you bitches, and my hair longer than yours and its natural. And what y'all niggas mad cause I caught you looking at my ass? Yea I thought so!" If anyone tried I would have fought them, but of course no one did. They sat there like children who had just been caught stealing cookies out of the cookie jar. No more problems out of them.

My 18th birthday was a blast. My mother was still being really cool and allowed all my friends to come over and celebrate with me. Cake and ice cream, cards, the radio and good conversation. I normally didn't do anything for my birthday, It felt really nice. With the arrival and departure of Christmas and New Years, I exhaled a deep sigh of relief. I was making honors and didn't have a single fight. Victory was literally right around the corner, 1997 was my year!

******

It was basketball season, and I made it a point to support my school at all the games, plays and performances. I hadn't been able to enjoy high school and because such activities would no longer be available to me, I attended everything. This particular game was the first time I really paid attention to the Drill Team. They were hot and rocked the house. I found myself mocking their movements while I was sitting in the bleachers. I was still a part of Espirit, but Drill Team did something we didn't. They danced, and I wanted to shake my ass and hair just like they did. I knew I could do it better anyway. After the performance, they sat in the audience with us.

One of the captains leaned into me and told me she saw me in the crowd. I was embarrassed but now was not the time for bashful blushing.

"No need to be shy. I know you're not. You can move that little body. Have you ever thought of joining the drill team?"

Was this really happening? Right here like this? "Of course I have, but I didn't know if men were allowed on the girls Unarmed Drill Team, and I have no desire to drill with the boys."

She laughed and smiled. "Well, West Side High has a boy on its team. We can go to Sergeant Cross, the drill instructor, tomorrow and see if he will let you join."

I was so excited. I couldn't even pay attention to the rest of the game. I was ready for tomorrow to be here. I told Angela and Keisha, and they supported the move. Jonathan told me I was perfect for it because I didn't care about the judgments anymore and to go do my thing.

The next day during lunch, the drill team captains and I went to the ROTC building and asked Sergeant Cross if I could join the team. He stared at me for a while like he was going to say no. We mentioned that West Side also had a male on their team. He said okay. He would have to clear it with our principal first, but he didn't see how it would be a problem. By the end of the day, I was the first boy in the history of Roosevelt High School to join a girl's drill team. I was definitely making a name for myself. Whether people hated me or loved me, they all knew who I was.

Moon was still the chorographer for the drill team, and was just as excited as me. I would go over to his house for extra practice, and before long, I had the entire drill down.

I couldn't wait to get on the big stage. March 17th was the annual step challenge held at West Side High School, and I knew I had to show up and show out! We had an early practice at the school at 6am, and by 11am we were headed to West Side High.

The show started at 1pm. When we arrived about 11:30 am, there were already people in the auditorium. There were five schools competing: West Side, Lew Wallace, Wirt, Horace Mann, and, of course Roosevelt and I heard it was sold out, all 5,000 seats. Nervous was an understatement. West Side won the year before and Roosevelt the year before that. We had to win. Our secret weapon was me. We were the only team with a male. I don't know what happen with West Side's boy. I honestly didn't care. With him out of the picture, all eyes would definitely be on my team and me. All my friends were coming, and their parents, and a few cousins: Evelena, Davida, and Nina, who attended West Side. She was holding me down at her school but mother was not there. We weren't arguing nearly as much. She still did not support me at all, especially doing this. She thought I was making a fool of myself and said everyone was going to laugh at me. I had to ignore her negativity. I wanted this. I was going to make sure I hit every step on every mark, just like I had practiced. I was going to bring down the house if it was the last thing I did.

Our school was second to compete. We had the biggest group that consisted of 39 girls and yours truly. We marched to the floor, and like the beat of the drums, my heart was pounding. I was nervous as hell but ready. I took the weave out, and my hair was all natural and swinging. I had a design cut in the back, and it was bumped hard. I was feeling myself. Moon had hooked me up. I looked around and everyone was on their feet. Some people looked shocked. I heard someone ask, "Is that a boy?" I just smiled. Angela and Keisha were right in the front and kept yelling my name. Talk about a serious adrenaline rush. Everyone was on the floor and we got into position. First with no music we did a screaming and stomping drill and the crowd was right there with us. Once the music dropped, it was complete pandemonium. I was so happy. I was doing something other gay boys wanted to do but were afraid to do. I had surpassed Moon's flamboyancy and was in my own lane. Everyone was going to know who I was.

The girls made a complete circle around me. We all put on our blindfolds. It was guillotine time. The crowd was going crazy. We tore up the floor and we marched off. I felt so accomplished. Complete precision and accuracy won us first place, and I was a part of it. I had set out to do something and completed the task. I was so proud of myself and my team.

I also had my very first modeling show senior year. I was unable to make the first one the initial year I joined because I was in jail, so this show meant a lot to me as well. Moon did my hair again. It was fierce. He gave me finger waves with glitter outlining the design in the back. Jonathan and I maintained a strong friendship after our detention center visit. He knew my financial situation and offered to buy my modeling clothes for the show because mother wouldn't. He got some nice things too! It was a major upgrade from my own wardrobe. My mother wasn't attending the show, but with the success of the drill team competition, I didn't care. My friends were going to be there, and, honestly, that was all that mattered. The show was a success. I felt amazing. Everything was so amazing.

School was like a different place. Once I couldn't stand to go. Now I couldn't stand to leave. My grades were outstanding. I was still on the honor roll. I had no fights, and my teachers loved me. I was trying my best to please my mother in any way I could, but she was not interested in anything I did. I couldn't worry about it. She had deep-rooted issues with herself, with me, and with life. On the other hand, I was finally smiling, really smiling. I was not, in any way, going to let her bring me down.

Prom was quickly approaching. Prom was the big dance, the ultimate party, the final hooray, and I didn't have the funds to go. I wasn't going to ask my mother for a dime. She knew that prom was coming and didn't say anything about it. I figured she didn't care, so why bring it up? One of the people I met through Moon, Terri, a transgender, said she would pay for everything including my tux, if she could be my date. I was down. I got to go to prom for free. I had a date, a way there, and I knew I would have a great time. I told the girls and Jonathan about it at lunch, and they said I was crazy and brushed me off. Someone must have been listening because as soon as third period started, the principal called into the class over the intercom and asked me to come to the office.

Mr. West, the principal, and Ms. Jones, the junior principal, were in his office when I arrived. They explained to me someone informed them I was bringing a drag queen to the prom. Well, I was, but a transgender. They didn't like the idea at all. Told me I already proved my point by drilling with the girls, and I didn't need to disrupt prom by attending with a drag queen. I explained my financial situation and the offer that lead me to bring a transgender to prom. She was giving me $500 to make sure I would be able to go. I had no problem with bringing her.

They asked me to wait in the hall. After a short discussion amongst themselves, they offered to pay for prom if I would take a real girl instead. I didn't even have to think about it. I said okay. They wrote me a check for $500. I felt like I was at the short end of the stick because I was missing an opportunity to make a statement. Showing up to prom with a drag queen really would have been priceless. I decided since they were trying to censor me, I would get my nails done the exact same way as my date, Lemeca, with French tips, and a ring finger design. Moon never failed when it was my time to make a statement. I had big ocean waves and pin curls with rhinestones all over my head. White and mint green were the colors of choice, and we looked amazing. To the school's surprise, Jonathan brought a drag queen and prom was still disrupted. Well, not really, she was beautiful and you could not tell she was a man, but everyone knew. It was a night of fun. There was no stress and no drama. PURE FUN!

******

Moon had me ripping and running with him the following day. I was exhausted when I got home only to find, SURPRISE! My mother had thrown me a surprise party and invited all my friends, classmates and people from the projects. The party was a blast. I was so happy. My mom actually took the time to do that for me. It was the first time I really felt like she cared and was proud of me.

GRADUATION TIME!

I sent out invitations to everyone. I wanted a packed audience and a lot of people to scream my name. I sent my dads; Robert, and biological father Pete, invitations. My aunts, grandmother, even Romie and his wife, got invitations. I was happy, and I wanted everyone to be happy with me. Everyone came minus my father. I don't know what he was doing, and I didn't care. I attempted to involve him in my life. He apparently didn't have time. No worries, my mother, Robert, aunts, cousins and everyone else came. It was perfect!

"Robert Theotis Edmond"

The crowd roared, and I was holding back tears of joy. I had done it. I made it. I completed the first half of my journey. I had never felt better. I walked across the stage to receive my diploma and as I went to shake "the principal's hand," he pulled me in and in a faint whisper said "congratulations" and smiled wide.

We partied hard that night I graduated. I was no longer a ward of the state and I felt free and alive. Terri, my mom's on again off again girlfriend, let me drive her Chrysler Sebring that night, and we all showed our asses.

It wasn't until mid-summer when Lester moved to Atlanta, Angela to Indiana State, Jonathan set out for adventure, and Michial was back and forth to Chicago. What was I was going to do? Everyone was gone or leaving. It was just Keisha and I. It was strange. In the beginning, Keisha and I didn't get along so well. Angela and I were the best of friends, but Angela and Keisha were best friends. The closer Angela and I got, the closer Keisha and I became. We grew even closer after Angela left because they had a fight about something, and neither of them wanted to kill it. Plus, we were friends. She was there, and so was I, we spent the entire summer together. All my family adored her. My mother loved her. Keisha was my life. We both got our driver's license that summer. Mother and Robert would let me use their cars to go anywhere. We got our hair done together. We went shopping. We were everywhere. It seemed all in vain though. She too was planning to leave at the end of the summer. She and my cousin "Black-Black" were in love and thought it would be cute to move to Indianapolis together while she went to school.

My world was turning upside down. What was I going to do? All my friends would really be gone. I started feeling sad, and people around me could tell. My grandmother Hazel believed in all sorts of things. S he said there was a prophetess at her church, and if I was so worried about what my future held, maybe I should go see her. I was interested but I was not going to go alone. I asked Keisha if she would come along. I met with her. First, she looked at me and said, "GOD bless." I returned the courtesy. She told me I would be moving soon, *(yeah, out of my mom's house),* out of town, and you are going to really make something of yourself. I see you setting out and accomplishing everything you want to do. You will be somewhat of a motivational speaker. She also told me that I would be able to see things as she saw them in my later years. I didn't know how to respond to her. Keisha was next. The Prophetess greeted her the same way and then told her she saw she'll be moving soon. She told her it was not a good move for her, but she had to do it. She was surrounded by people that loved her as well, and things would be okay.

On the way home, Keisha started shaking. She said the Prophetess really scared her. I laughed it off and told her I didn't believe that old lady, and she shouldn't either. She said I was going to be a motivational speaker. Come on now, we know I am not doing that.

The morning of September 28, 1997, Keisha came and picked me up so we could go to a few stores and get some things for her new apartment. We rode around talking and laughing. I knew she had to go, but my gut was telling me not to let her. She was smiling and so excited. I just let the thought go. I didn't want to spoil her mood. That night was hard for me. Keisha and "Black-Black" were officially packed and ready to go to Indiana University Perdue University Indianapolis (IUPUI) College Indianapolis, Indiana. I had to be happy for her. She was smart and going off to college. She'd be home soon.

She was not a very affectionate person, but she did give me a big tight hug. I was so sad I never wanted to let her go. "I love you Keisha."

"I'm not no dike, but I will always love you too."

I started crying.

"Stop all that. I'll be back on your birthday."

She got in the car.

******

I started taking classes at Ivy Tech State College. Life was slow for a minute, but I wasn't alone anymore. Michial was back. Then Lester came back from Atlanta and brought Moon back around. Things were fun again. "Black-Black" came home for Thanksgiving alone. I was confused. Keisha and I spoke just about every day, so I was of course surprised that he was here. She didn't tell me he was coming. He said he needed a break and was going back after he ate some good food and chilled out. I knew Keisha loved my cousin. I really hoped he hadn't done anything dumb to break her heart while he was there. He may have been my cousin, but she was my sister, and I cared if she was okay.

Thanksgiving morning the phone rang, "Hello?"

"Hey, baby."

The voice was dry and low, but I knew it was Keisha. "Hey girl, how are you? Why didn't you tell me "Black-Black" was coming home without you?

I heard her cough and changed my line of questioning, "Keisha where are you?"

"The hospital."

"The hospital!? The hospital for what?"

"My blood count was low, but I'm okay. I just wanted to say Happy Thanksgiving. I will definitely be home for your birthday."

I didn't know how to feel. I was nervous. *Her blood count? Isn't that only affected if you're sick?*

"Robert, I love you!"

I immediately started crying. I knew something was wrong. "I love you too, girl."

We hung up.

I ran to find "Black-Black," and when I did I was mad; more sad or confused but definitely angry. I asked him what was going on with Keisha. I told him she just told me she was in the hospital because her blood count was low. I wanted to know what that meant. I was in no way prepared for what he told me. Apparently, there was never a school. Keisha left and went directly to the hospital. She was on medication to make her better. She was going to be okay. He was honest with me and told me she looked bad. That's why he left. He couldn't stand to see her sick the way she was. I was so sad for my friend. I was wondering why she didn't tell me and if Angela knew.

It was twelve days before my 19th birthday. Everyone was coming home for Christmas break. I was planning a nice time for all my friends.

Late evening, I got the call from Lacey. She was Keisha's best friend, and mother to my godson. Keisha was gone. Okay. Keisha was gone where? I couldn't really comprehend it at first. I had spoken to Keisha just a few days ago. I wanted to pick up the phone and call her. Better yet, I wanted to drive to Indianapolis and see her. Ask her, where she went? I couldn't, and I wouldn't be able to ever again. I almost dropped out of college. The pain was unbearable. I was devastated. When she died, part of my soul died with her. She protected me all those years when she was the one who needed protection. I was a complete mess. I figured out what death actually was when she died. It meant no more—never again; never-ever again unless you die too.

Keisha had Leukemia and told my family she was sick. I also found out the reason she was home schooled the last few months of senior year was to receive her treatment. I just lost my other half. She was here one day and gone the next. I was so blind. I didn't even realize she was sick the entire time.

Mother was my backbone and by my side through the entire ordeal. She consoled me daily and eased my pain, as a parent should when a child hurts.

******

As I look back now, I have finally accepted Keisha's death. She had suffered so much even as a child. Her mother had beaten her and mistreated her as well. Keisha ended up living with her grandmother who raised her until she died.

CHAPTER TWELVE

DL MEN

O h my, oh my, was that really my life? The things I remembered; I couldn't shake my past. There would be times I would get lost in thought wondering how I did the things I did, and why I was the way I was. Remembering my molestation definitely clarified many things for me. I wondered why and how I was able to be an escort. I wondered why I was attracted to the kind of men I chose. The dreams were still coming, and a flood of unwanted memories were floating around in my head. My life, my life, my life.

******

Spring was my favorite time of year as a child. I loved the flowers on the trees and how bright and fresh everything was. It was simply beautiful, unlike the darkness of my life. Not even a life changing experience could get my family to pay attention to me. I was still home alone a lot. Romie was doing his thing. My mother was working. Neither one was worried about Robert. The excitement behind Bob (my molester) wasn't even fully digested before my second cousin was making himself comfortable. He stayed in the projects and was always over our house. He was related, so he had access to our house and Aunt Sylvia's just about any time of the day. He was 15, and we were semi-close. I was 11-years old, and the closest thing I'd felt to affection was Bob. When my cousin started showing an interest in me, I was happy. I wanted someone to care, and he was there. He asked me questions I didn't know how to answer. He wanted to know when Bob touched me? How did he touch me? Where? I didn't want to tell him what happened, so I usually ignored him, and I think it was my silence about that situation that led him to believe if he was with me it would never get out. He was hanging at the house while mother was at work and started grinding on me. I could feel his penis get erect. I was nervous. He told me it was okay and he'd be nice. He removed his pants first and then mine. He covered his penis in Vaseline and worked his penis into my buttock. This was the first time I had sex. Bob only used his fingers. I didn't know how to respond to the feeling. I felt obligated to do it because he was spending so much time with me. So I did. He was really gentle. It became a regular thing.

Another one of my second cousins, who I'd never met before, came to visit for the summer. He was country and smelled like pot-pourri. He was 15 years old and had a big penis. He told me he knew I was open, and he wanted some. I didn't know what he was talking about until he pulled my pants down and started having sex with me; it hurt so badly. His penis was much bigger than my other cousin's. I didn't like it at all. He made me feel nasty and used. I didn't even know him. He thought it was okay to touch me. He tried to make it a regular thing, but I was still having sex with my other cousin so I tried to avoid him. I thought they would find out I was doing this with both of them and get mad at me. It was becoming a lot to handle. I was only 11 and I had sex with both of them in the same day because they were making me. If I said no, they would ask questions. So I just did what they wanted. My country second cousin left at the end of the summer, I was so happy. My other cousin didn't want to stop and I really didn't want to either, It made me feel wanted so I wanted it to continue. We kept having sex for almost a year. Something about what was going on didn't sit right with me, but none of the adults in my life said anything to the contrary, so I went with it. By the time I was 12 years old, I didn't know what was going on or how I felt about anything.

******

Alex McKinney had a lot of other brothers and sisters and a lot of toys. He was 15, and hung out with Romie. He knew what was happening to me. He was the neighborhood bully. He had everyone scared of him, but he was very nice to me. He would invite me over to his house to play with his toys. He had all kinds of toys. Alex was very attractive. He was toasted caramel with a muscular body, 5' 7", and a low cut fade. I was over his house in the living room playing with the toys. He stood in front of me and pulled his penis out. It was big and with defined veins and a curve. He played with himself, and then asked me to hold it and stroke it for him. I did and his penis got very hard. He wanted me to put it in my mouth. I did. He told me I needed to open my mouth wider because I was biting him. This was my second time performing oral sex. After a while he didn't have to tell me to stop biting his penis. I only gave Alex head. We never had sex. I got so good at it, and started enjoying it so much, that I made sure if I liked someone I did it to them.

At the same time Maurice "Munk" Moody caught my eye, and I caught his attention. He stayed on the right side of DuSable Arms. That's where most of the cutest boys stayed. We lived on the left side. I wanted Monk more than Alex hands down. He was attractive with a muscular build, caramel skin tone, a low cut fade and nasty sexy bow leg. He was the oldest of three. He had a little sister and brother. Before long, I was giving Monk head. He was 15-years old. I had just turned 12-years old. Troy, my little cousin, walked in the bedroom at Aunt Sylvia's and saw me giving Monk head. I was so nervous. Monk ran out of the house. I knew Troy was going to tell on me. My mother came home and we went to Monk's house to confront him. We both denied anything happened. The situation was left alone. To my surprise, my mother didn't beat me. Instead, she gave away all my toys that my grandmother bought me to the kids in DuSable Arms. She said that was what happened when people lied. They got things taken away from them. It made me very sad.

Alex was furious when he found out about Monk. He asked me if I wanted to play on a scooter. He was going to tie it to the back of his bike and make it go really fast. I didn't know his kindness towards me turned into hatred until he then took off as fast as he could. I held on for dear life.

Before I knew it, he turned a corner so fast that the scooter flipped over, and I was dragged a couple feet. The skin on my right buttock cheek burned completely off and ants were all over me. I couldn't stop crying. The pain was unbearable. I cried the entire walk home and Alex didn't care. He broke it off with me soon after that.

I was okay with that because I really liked Monk. He had a girlfriend and side girls, but he still called me over. Our first time together was like nothing I'd ever experienced. I was indeed a virgin, and he was my first. Yes, I was penetrated by both my second cousins, but he wasn't family and I really wanted him. He was gentle but really worked me out. I wanted him to be with me all the time. I hated that he wasn't gay like me. He gave me money all the time. Whatever I asked for I could have. The only thing I had to do was keep my business to myself, and I did. He continued to love me slow until I was 15 years old. There was no one that made me feel like he did. But I was sharing and he was too. I only had sex with one other person while I was with him. I was giving head because I enjoyed it, and he wasn't always around.

******

It was as if everyone knew my family's schedule. Almost every day after school it seemed as if another guy was approaching me. Michael Moore was one of Romie's friends. He lived on the right side of DuSable Arms. He was the middle child of five kids. He came looking for Romie. I told him Romie was not home. He asked if he could use the restroom, and I let him in. He sat down on the couch and started talking about nothing. He then pulled down his pants and told me to suck his penis. The tone of his voice made me feel like I didn't have a choice in the matter. So I did. He made a lot of noises I had not heard before. He was really relaxed. Later in the evening Michael came back and brought a friend with him. Stacey was one of the neighborhood dope boys, so he knew Romie too. Stacey Ray was very skinny and tall, light skinned, and he had a goatee. He had multiple brothers and sisters. Michael and Stayla "Stacey-Ray" DeWitt wanted me give both of them head, one after the other. I didn't know what I was doing. I was in the sixth grade.

After they were done, they both gave me some money, left and never asked me for anything again.

Mother moved us to Aetna, Indiana in the fall of '91 when she married Tony, but I was still spending time in DuSable Arms. My cousin's girlfriend's twin brother, Anthony McGee, was another friend of Romie's. Romie wasn't hitting me anymore, but he still

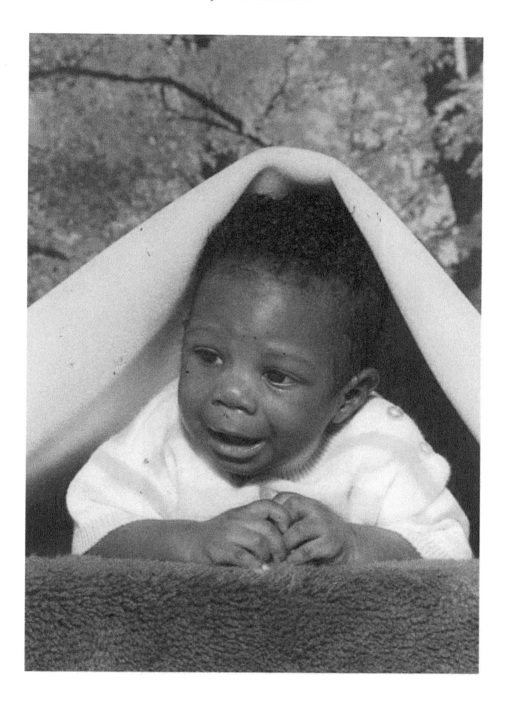

was calling me names. He did this all in front of everyone. So the entire housing project knew all kinds of things they should have never known about me. Anthony came over. I told him Romie wasn't home. He decided he would wait for him to get back.

I didn't care what he was doing. I was worried about my own life. "So what do you do in here all day?"

"Homework." I was twelve, what did he expect me to say? He looked at me like he knew different, so I paid him no mind.

"You ever watched a porno?"

I thought about my answer and where this was going but still answered honestly. "Yes."

"You ever see one with two men?"

"No"

"Let's go in the bedroom. I'll show you how they do things."

No one was that forward with me before. We went into the back room. He pulled down his pants and mine as well. He bent me over and put his mouth on my butt and started licking it. It was strange and very wet. I wanted him to stop. I didn't like it at all. Then he put Vaseline on his penis and pushed himself into me. His penis was thicker than Monk's, but I liked Monk's better. He was the fourth person to penetrate me and the second that wasn't family. We had sex two more times in two weeks, before I moved in with my dad, Robert. Neither time was that magnificent. Living with my dad made having sex easy because he was never home.

Monk use to come over all the time and get me good in the basement. He had a very healthy appetite and didn't allow me to make excuses or be lazy ever. I was 14 when I left my dad's and moved back to DuSable Arms. Monk's family moved out of the projects and into a house. It didn't stop us from seeing each other. I would walk to his house, or he would come get me but we made sure to see each other. He taught me many different things and even things I wasn't ready to learn. Monk was a street nigga, a thug, and in a gang. He was 18 when he was sent to jail. I did what any other person would do. I moved on to the next person.

I liked the guys I dealt with. They weren't like me, none of them. They were all straight and hardcore. I soon learned that it wasn't just a secret I was protecting for these guys but an entire lifestyle. They were considered men on the "Down-Low" (DL). They would do anything to protect their secrets. I was turning project niggas out left and right and got everything I wanted in return. Everyone knew who my brother was and I used that to my advantage.

******

I was selling weed for some girls who stayed in my building when I really noticed Antonio "Coop" Davis. He was Michael Moore's older brother tall chocolate and bow-legged. All the girls loved him. His body was crazy. I was walking around the projects selling weed and chilling when Coop and his best friend, "Double G," asked me to ride with them and smoke a blunt. I only hit the blunt a couple of times, and I was higher then I'd ever been. To my surprise, it was a primo blunt. Meaning it was laced it with cocaine. They were super cool and Coop's demeanor was so aggressive it really made me want him. I could tell both "Coop" and "Double G" wanted me. "Double G" was fine too. He was 5'7 with an athletic build. He was a caramel like Brach's candy with brown eyes, a low dark fade. I was so high when they dropped me off that it felt like I was floating to my front door.

The next evening after school the phone rang and it was for me, "Lil' Rob, What you doing?"

"Nothing"

"What is your aunt doing?"

"Sleeping." I was listening hard, trying to figure out who it was.

"Are you coming back outside?"

I realized it was Coop. "No, it's late."

"I know, but I want to taste your hole and show you something."

I was instantly hard. I was turned on for real. "What am I getting out of this?"

He was the top drug dealer. I knew he had whatever I wanted.

He asked me what I wanted so I told him money. He agreed and told me where to meet him.

I walked into the apartment and into the dark room. I couldn't see anything. All of a sudden I felt a cold object on the back of my head. Coop had a gun to my head. With a calm yet intense tone, he proclaimed, "If you tell anyone, I will fucking kill you."

I assured him he had nothing to worry about and to relax.

We removed our pants. He laid me on my back and pulled up my legs until my ass was in the air. I didn't know what he was about to do, but I was ready for it. He started with small pecks around my cheeks. He took his tongue and licked my hole. He licked it up and down and in circles. He stuck his tongue in and out of my ass. It felt amazing. My nipples started to get hard. My penis was a rock. I was enjoying every move his tongue made. Then he stood up and let his dick dangle in my face. It was nice. I put it in my month. His knees got weak. He said he wanted to feel me and made me stop. He lifted my legs in the air again and slid his penis inside. He was filling and felt amazing. He was rough and gentle, mad and happy. He had his way with me. No one had done it like that before. My penis was so hard it hurt. I touched myself and ejaculated all over the bed. The feeling was beyond words. I was embarrassed. He was the fifth person I had had sex with, and that had never happened before. I think he could see it on my face. He started talking dirty to me, which turned me on even more. I was glad when he came because he fucked long and hard. I was exhausted. He gave me $300 and I left the apartment.

The entire walk home I thought about it. It was so good. He made me nut. That was a completely new feeling. I was in love.

A couple weeks later "Double G" asked me to meet him outside. It was a very hot night. He pulled up to the apartments playing with himself and looking at me like I was a steak or something. He asked if I was ready to take a ride. My response was yes, as usual. I knew what was about to happen. We pulled up to Ironwood Park, and he pulled down his pants. He put my head-game to the test when he asked if I could make him cum before we got back to Martin Luther King Street. That was almost two miles round trip, down to Ivy Tech and back. I didn't think that would be a problem. He pulled off, and I started doing my thing. His penis was small so it was easy to suck. I could move faster. He was clenching his ass and grabbing my head the entire ride. Like a perfectly cooked turkey, when we approached MLK, he was done! He took me home. We never did anything again. "Coop" was who I wanted. He did me right, and for almost five years, he continued to do so.

******

My memories were haunting me everywhere I turned. Sleeping, taking a shower, driving, when I had sex, even when I looked in the mirror. I couldn't escape my past. I lived it everyday. I made it seem like escorting was such a dirty deed, but I had been doing it all my life. I was twelve and having sex with 16 and 17 year old guys. *Wasn't that rape? Molestation? Didn't that make them pedo-*

philes? Something? Even if I did agree, they were grown. They knew better than I did. I was sick. I locked myself in the room. I wasn't accepting any calls and didn't answer Nina's knocks. I felt nasty, dirty and disgusted with myself. I wanted people to respect me, but here I was allowing myself to be misused and disrespected. I did not know what to do.

I heard the clap of thunder and saw the lightening light the sky. I wanted to be outside. I threw on some clothes and tiptoed out the house heading towards the Pontiac. I just sat there at first. I didn't know what I wanted to do, so I got on highway 35W towards the south side. I had no intended destination. I just wanted to go somewhere away from where I was.

"No More Drama" by Mary J. Blige was on repeat. It was one of my favorite CD's. All of the songs touched me and made me hate myself for the way I had allowed people to treat me; hate others for the way they treated me; feel some kind of way about GOD for letting it all happen to me. I did not want to live anymore because the pain was just unbearable. The rain was coming down like rocks on my windshield. I closed my eyes and pressed down on the gas pedal. Even with my eyes closed I could see bright flashing lights. Horns were honking. I kept driving. I opened my eyes and was sitting on the shoulder.

GOD had a different plan for me. It wasn't my time.

CHAPTER THIRTEEN

FROM ROBERT TO SAMUEL

I looked up and I was near the 35th/36th Street exit in south Minneapolis. My cousin Felicia stayed off of that exit. I got out the car into the pouring rain and cried the entire way to Felicia's front door. It was a little after 11pm. I didn't want to disturb her, but I needed a friend. She came to the door, and I just continued to cry. "Robert, what is wrong?"

I couldn't catch my breath. My life was a gigantic mess.

"Sit down." She handed me a tissue and took my car keys. "Where are you coming from? It's Tuesday night. What are you doing on this side?"

I calmed down enough to tell her what I tried to do. She turned my body toward hers and grabbed my face,

"It is not the end of the world Robert. Why would you try something so selfish? You know this family loves you. All is being worked out with the past, but it's the past. You can't let it control you and hold you back. You have to keep your head up. Follow the stars not the clouds. You have nieces, a nephew, cousins, a mother and father, brother, sister, and friends. Come on now. Let's just chill. No time for negative thinking. I love you!"

She was right. There was more to me than a horrible past. I had an amazing future. I'd been in Minnesota four years now. I remember when I was told I was going to take this trip. I didn't believe the Prophetess that day, but look. Here I am. That meant my platform was bigger than my dreams, and I was ready to attack it head on.

We ended the night lying across the couch watching *Food Network* and sharing laughs. The next morning I felt alive and refreshed! I knew that it was time for some serious change. It had to start with me.

✶✶✶✶✶✶

Summer was approaching and Jonathan announced that domestic travel was over. We were now going international. I was hesitant after 9/11, but he assured me they'd beefed up security. We were free to move about the world.

I picked up a passport application and looked over the list of documents I needed to complete the process. I found my birth certificate a week later and noticed the "Father's Signature" space was not signed. I stared at it awhile before I decided to call my mom. I wanted to know why it wasn't signed. She answered the phone with an attitude. She was upset because she was calling me, and I wasn't answering or returning any of her calls. I honestly just didn't want to be bothered, but I had a question only she could answer. I had to call. I asked her why no one signed my birth certificate. I knew Robert wasn't my real father. He was there, Why didn't he sign? If my father knew you were pregnant, why didn't he sign? He could have still been an absentee father. She retold the story of my conception and the deception. I really didn't care about the story. I had already heard it. I wanted my father's name on my birth certificate.

I felt like a bastard child. She told me she signed it. So my quarrel was with someone else, and she was getting off the phone.

She was so rude. 219-933-9000...

"Hello."

I thought he would never answer, "Hey dad, it's Robert"

His voice sounded a little more chipper. "Hey son. How are you doing? What's going on?"

"Well, I was looking at my birth certificate and noticed the "Father's Signature" space wasn't signed. It makes me feel like a bastard. I know who my father is. I want his name on my birth certificate."

He was cool with it. "Go to the court house and find out what we have to do to change it. I'll pay any fees associated. Robert?"

"Yes?"

"Would you take my last name?"

Oh my goodness. I was happy. I couldn't have planned a better turnout for this conversation. Of course I wanted my father's last name. "Yes, I would love to have your last name."

"Well, what would you say to taking my full name, if I asked you to?"

"Samuel Percy Holloway, III? I would be honored to be the third."

I was super ecstatic. This was just what I needed. A new start would start with my name change. I loved my dad Robert, but I hated that my molester carried the name as well. Robert was a past not forgotten, but left in its time. My father said he would pay any applicable fees, and he was happy I would have his name. Pete may have been an absentee father, but I felt like he was extending a hand. I had to reach back. I wanted a new start. He did too. Together we were taking steps to a forgiving future.

I called the courthouse the following day. I was informed that name changing was not an overnight process nor was having my birth certificate signed. Pete had to hand write a letter; have it notarized and send it to the judge explaining that he was my father and wanted to sign the birth certificate. He would have to indicate he was the originator of the name change idea. After the paperwork was reviewed, I would be notified if I would have a hearing date, or if the case would be closed. The documentation was completed and sent in. All I could do was wait.

******

Grandpa Holloway died May 17, 2002. My father paid for my plane ticket, so I could make it to Gary for the funeral. I caught the earliest flight I could find. I couldn't believe there was snow on the ground. Lana, my mother's new girlfriend, picked me up from the airport and took me to their house.

After I got dressed, mother and I went to my grandparent's house where everyone was meeting. I was nervous. Besides my grandparents, I knew none of my father's relatives. I didn't know how they would respond to me. I was 23 and gay. I was not flamboyant gay, but people knew. I was a nephew everyone, young and old, would be meeting for the first time.

There was a lady standing in the door when we pulled up. When I walked to the door, she asked who I was.

"I'm your brother's son, Robert."

She was staring at me awkwardly. It was like she didn't even hear what I said. "I know who you are. You look just like my brother."

She reached out and pulled me into a warm and welcoming hug. I felt great. The first person I met embraced me. That gave me a little hope.

I saw Grandma Holloway as soon as I walked into the house. I gave her a big hug, and she immediately started crying. I was looking around for my father when he emerged from the kitchen. It had been five years or so since I last saw him. It was like I was looking into a mirror. He walked over and gave me a big fatherly hug. He was happy I made it. I was too.

Mother drove to the funeral. It was a nice ceremony. My grandfather was a respectable man and many people came out to pay "their respect" to him. Later that evening, everyone met at Aunt Kate's house in Aetna, Indiana. A few of us were sitting in the living room when Aunty asked my last name. I wasn't sure how to answer. I was in the middle of a name change, so that's what I told her. Edmond was my last name, but I was changing my name entirely from Robert T. Edmond to Samuel P. Holloway, III. I met a few cousins I went to school with. It was strange, but I was having a great time. I had a lot more family immediately around me than I thought.

******

Bye-bye weekend, and hello 9 to 5. I missed the money I made escorting, but I had to leave that part of my life alone. I was doing very well. There was no need to be greedy. I received a correspondence from the court about my name change while at Grandpa Holloway's funeral. When I opened it, there was only good news. On June 3, 2002, I had a scheduled hearing. That's exactly what I wanted. Now I could go in front of a judge, and explain to him or her why I wanted this name change. I had a good feeling I was going to get it. The hearing was only two weeks away. I requested my time off and made sure I was well prepared.

On my way to the district court I was a mess. I was nervous, excited, and a little strange. This was my name we were changing.

There were so many pros and cons. People wouldn't be able to find me. That would be great for people I didn't want to find me. What about friends I just happen to lose touch with? What if they wanted to find me? I would have to change all of my formal documentation. That meant a lot of paperwork and waiting again! I would be able to start fresh. I wanted a much more subtle, and laid back lifestyle, someone to love, and a home. Did I really want to tell everyone I had two fathers or the situation about my birth certificate? Was that anyone's business?

There was no street parking and the garage was $10. I met with the judge in his office. We conference called my father, and were both sworn in. The very first question was directed towards my father. The judge asked him if he wanted a paternity test. I smiled when he stated he knew I was his son. That would not be necessary. He asked a few questions in regards to our current relationship. How often we spoke? Seen each other? How close I was with the family? Things like that. I was nervous. I didn't know if that would have any real bearing on his ultimate decision. We were not the father and son duo I would have liked us to be, but we were working on it. I felt that was what truly mattered.

The judge must have felt the same. He granted me a full name change and ordered my father's name added to my birth certificate. Before long, every important piece of documentation, and all my work information displayed my "shiny" new name. I was Samuel Percy Holloway, III and most importantly, I had a "Father's Signature" on my birth certificate.

My mother was pissed I changed my name and didn't consult with her first. She told me I had no right. She gave me that name. That's what she wanted to call her son. She felt like I had changed it and didn't bother to think about how she would feel. I tried to explain hurting her was unintentional. I was going to change my last name, but my father offered me the entire name. I wanted to take it. I was still her son no matter what my name was, and I was going to love her exactly the same. She didn't care about any of that. I betrayed her by changing my name without asking. She'd call me "Samuel" only when, and if, she decided to call me "Samuel." There was just no pleasing her. I was leaving all the petty drama in 2002. My name was "Samuel P. Holloway, III" now. She'd just have to accept that.

CHAPTER FOURTEEN

ADONIS

The New Year started with new energy. On January 12, 2003, LaShenia gave birth to a beautiful, fat-faced, curly haired little girl, Kayla. I was happy to have another niece. That definitely meant I had to make my way to California. I couldn't have my nieces growing up without me. I didn't have anyone serious in my life. Sometimes I wanted it. Other times I thought it'd be a burden. I had my boys who had their girls. I was fine with that. As long as they were DL, they weren't too worried about my whereabouts. That was all I wanted. Good sex with no strings. By July, I was singing a different tune.

Deep dark waves with Timberland boots and jeans. He wore a clean white tee, covering 195 pounds of red bone heaven. He was slim smooth and looked very athletic. I wanted to know who he was before he was completely in the credit union. He was with a pregnant woman and a little boy. The boy looked just like him, so I assumed that was his family. What a shame. He was very attractive. I watched them out of the corner of my eye until they were gone. I was a little upset they didn't come to my window, and just that fast he was gone.

122

A few weeks later, he came in to make an early morning deposit. He was smiling and laughing while he was in line. I wanted to know what was funny. I worked the line, so he would be serviced by my window, so I could ask. He seemed shy and bashful when he got to the counter. I thought it was cute and remarked that I wanted to laugh as well. I asked what was so funny. He ignored me and kept smiling. I got irritated. I thought he was trying to be funny and immature because I was gay. I just wanted to get him away from my window. I finished his transaction, gave him a receipt and told him to have a nice day. He didn't leave. He stood there and started writing on the receipt. There were other people in line behind him. That irritated me even more. I told him to step aside, so I can help the people behind him. He slid his receipt to me and turned it so I could read it.

I thought he was about to rob me. To my surprise, the note said, "I think I'm bi. Don't tell anybody."

That was the only thing on the paper. I was happy. He was fine as hell, and I was highly attracted to him. I asked him for his number. Again, he ignored me and walked out of the credit union. Damn.

I knew he would come back. I was prepared when he did. My face lit up when I saw him in the line. I worked the line again, so that I would be the teller to service him. When he got to the window, I slid him a small piece of paper that read. "Let me help you make that decision, 612-555-1212."

He smiled at me. We finished his transaction, and he was out the door. He called that evening, and we stayed on the phone for hours. He told me everything about his life. His name was Adonis, and he was half black and half Italian. He was 22-years old and moved to Minneapolis from New York. He'd been home from Iraq for a few months and had his little girl, Rachael, two weeks earlier.

He lived with his fiancé and his five-year-old son, a junior from a previous relationship. He had full custody. He was playing the stay-at-home dad role, while taking online classes and was looking for people to kick it with. When we discovered how close we stayed to each other, I knew we were going to be friends. He was only two exits up from Nina and me. I was in need of a new friend; he was a new friend indeed.

He asked many questions pertaining to my life outside of the credit union. He asked questions that gave him insight on how I dressed, wore my hair, carried myself and the company I kept. I knew exactly what he was doing. He wanted to feel me out. Adonis had a girl and a family. He wanted to make sure if he did go down that road with me, I wasn't easily "clockable." We made plans to chill the next evening and ended our call.

Adonis was very cautious. He didn't want to be introduced to anyone I knew too soon because he didn't know if he was going to be around me long. He came to me and Nina's and went straight to my room. We talked some more. Our conversation was mostly him asking the same questions from the night before. We smoked a couple of blunts. He expressed his feelings towards me. He confessed, I was the first man he was attracted to. He really wanted me. He asked me what I was down to do. I was down for whatever he was down for. He'd never been with a man before. I wanted to make sure he did it again, so we could do anything he wanted.

I turned the lights off and the TV up. We got undressed, and I was happy. His dick was big. He started eating me out. For a beginner, he was the bomb. He then put on a Magnum condom. He was so gentle. It was like making love when he slid inside of me. When I heard him exhale I knew he liked the way I felt. He caressed me slow. Something I was not used to. I came twice, and we didn't even change from missionary position. He was holding me tight and biting into my shoulder. He was an amazing lover. I walked him to the bathroom when we were finished and washed him off. His face was so different. He looked pleased. I liked it.

The following evening we went to the mall. He said if I was going to be with him I needed to be 100 percent "unclockable". He bought me my first pair of Timberland boots. My jeans needed to fit a little looser. My shirts needed to be a little bigger. He changed my hoop earnings to diamond studs.

We became Cheech and Chong and were inseparable. I had hair and was not cutting it. He decided he would cut his. He didn't want any reason for anyone to look at us as anything but friends. I was fine with that. He treated me right, so I treated him well. Before long, I was a mini-me Adonis, masculine and "unclockable".

We went to clubs together, movies and the mall. We ate together, showered together, and slept together. We were together almost five days a week. His fiancé was a nurse at the hospital. I knew her schedule like I worked it. On the nights that she worked the late shift, I spent the night and left early, right before she came home. On my days off, I was at Adonis's place cooking, cleaning, washing clothes, and taking care of their children. Rachael was the sweetest baby. She hardly cried and was easy to put to sleep. Adonis Jr. was rambunctious and lively. We used to play all the time.

Adonis would be on the couch with his hands in his pants. I would sit beside him with the baby. Some days I thought it was wrong. These weren't my kids. He wasn't MY MAN, but I wasn't lying. I loved everything about him. I wanted nothing more than to be with him. My family liked him. The boys didn't know about us. They thought he was just a friend. I made the relationship sound so good to the girls; they wanted me to stay with him. Adonis was my life. I'd changed my whole demeanor for him. I played along with him. I was his homeboy and booty on the side. I loved him in my life. I smiled more, laughed lots and was, believe it or not, only having sex with him. He didn't want to share me, even though I was sharing him. But I understood. It was two completely different things—him with us and me or her with someone else. She had her lane. I had mine. It was just a matter of time before he was completely in mine.

I knew Adonis was going to leave April for me. I'd completely turned him out. He would do anything for me. One night coming home from the club I put on a deep voice and said, "Suck my dick!" He did for twenty minutes. He gave ME head for the entire ride home. He wanted to make sure he satisfied all my needs and asked me if I wanted to fuck him instead, one night. I was usually turned off at the thought of my man being a bottom. I wanted Adonis, and he let me have it. I'm not going to lie. It felt good. The head and his butt were amazing, but I was too lazy for top work. I was the girl. That was the only time we did that. He made sure I was fly, never hungry and always right. He even opened a second account for me that he automatically deposited almost $800 into every month. He was my homey, my top homey. We spent Christmas and New Years together. I was on a cloud entering 2004. Everything was taken care of. He was really my lover and best friend.

******

It was a beautiful spring day. I'd just gotten out of the bed with my man and was on my way to work, smiling. The day was just getting started when April's mother walked in carrying Rachael. I did not want to talk to that lady. I tried to divert the line. Damn, my technique hadn't worked this go round. She was standing in my face. I tried to finish her transaction, as quickly as possible. Rachael was reaching for me and started to cry. April's mother asked if I knew her daughter or granddaughter. She was trying to calm Rachael down when she stated the only people Rachael went to or cried for were herself, Rachael's mother, or her father. She never went to strange men.

I kept my head down until the transaction was complete. I told her I didn't know her, her daughter or the baby and to have a nice day. I was nervous. One of the other tellers noticed how often Adonis came to the credit union, and how he would only come to my window and asked me about us. I didn't confirm anything, but women talk. Another teller was April's friend. They always talked whenever she came into the credit union. I figured someone said something to her. I knew they knew something because all eyes were on me while April's mother was at my window. I didn't have time for confrontation and drama, but I was going to get it.

The following afternoon April came to the credit union. She had Rachael with her. My palms began to sweat. I started working the line so that I wouldn't get her. The day was still young, and I couldn't handle this right now. She was "ill-will" mugging me the entire time she was in line. I could feel her eyes burning through me. Whenever I looked up, they were right there. I was still on a transaction when April was up. Lucky me, the next teller was free. Wrong! April looked directly at me and let someone in front of her.

"I'm waiting for him!" she said.

My heart dropped. I was nervous as hell. I kept repeating, *Sam just be calm. Play it cool. She'll never know. Babies can't talk.* Talk about a mudslide. I look up and Adonis Jr. is walking into the credit union with his grandma. April walked to the counter, and A.J. saw me. He yelled, "What's up little dude?!" That's what he called me because we didn't want him to know my name. I was in the twilight zone. *(::plays Twilight Zone music::)*

April leaned into the counter and asked me if I knew her children. I stood there speechless. What could I have possibly said? She was mad. She looked at A.J., and told him to tell her how he knew me. I could have died. A.J. told her I cooked for him. I played with him, and I slept with daddy. Oh shit! He actually knew the truth. Rachel was reaching for me and crying. I didn't know what to do. She knew I was gay. Adonis was busted. The star witness was his five-year-old son. I excused myself from my window and stayed in the back until I knew she was gone.

Making matters that much tenser, Adonis was calling my job every 30 minutes. I couldn't take the calls. I was at work. My day had already been severely spoiled. He left messages to call him. Said it was urgent. I already knew the urgency. I honestly didn't know what to tell him. I didn't know what to do.

I called Adonis when I got off work. Told him I was leaving the credit union, and meet me at the house if he wanted to talk. I thought about him and April the entire drive. I loved Adonis. We'd been together nine months. I'd never dealt with anyone that long. He was strong and stable. The sex was great. Our friendship was amazing, but I knew it was about to be over. Adonis was DL. He wasn't about to take me home and run down the streets with me. He was waiting for me outside the house when I pulled up. We went inside. He explained April found out about us, but had no hard proof, so he denied her allegations. She didn't care. She didn't trust him. She put him and A.J out. He asked if he could stay with me. I liked our relationship. I knew I cared for him more than I'd ever cared for any man, but I could not do that. He could not stay with me. I didn't even stay by myself.

He said it was cool. There were no hard feelings. He left. I never saw him again.

******

A month or so later, April came into the credit union. I hadn't seen her in awhile. I thought she was using a different branch to avoid seeing me. She came in, walked straight to my window and excused herself to the person standing there. She leaned in and asked to speak with me when I was done with the customer. I was scared. She was calm as hell. I thought she was going to kill me or jump on me for real. She stepped to the window when the lady walked away. She asked if she could speak with me later after work. She said she needed to talk. She wanted to have the talk directly with me. At first I thought she was trying to set me up, but she really didn't seem angry. I gave her my number and told her to call me later.

Talk about timing, April called as soon as I walked in the door. She didn't want to talk over the phone. She wanted to go out and have drinks. It was Friday night, and the "Quest" was supposed to be jumping, so I agreed to go. I had to play it safe. I was driving. She was at her mom's and gave me the address and directions. I acted like I was taking them down but wasn't. I knew exactly where I was going. I got dressed in an orange DKNY wife-beater, white shorts, and my white mid top Air Force Ones.

I pulled in front of the house, and my jaw dropped. I was in utter disbelief. We were dressed alike! She had on an orange shirt that tied in the front, white shorts, and white stiletto sandals. She looked beautiful. I knew why she and Adonis were together. They truly complimented each other. When she got in the car, she immediately started laughing and clapping her hands. We high-fived.

April looked, and said we look good as hell. We rode into down-town high on our heads. It was like we were old friends, singing together and dogging men. It made me forget the original reason we were together.

The line for Quest was wrapped around the corner. That meant it was going to be packed. Just what I wanted. April treated me to drinks. After my second one, I was done. She kept on drinking. She wanted to get out, have fun, and dance the night away. People were complimenting our outfits all night. Boys and girls were hit-ting on us. There was no tension, and I liked that. April was so cool. I almost felt bad for sleeping with Adonis.

On the ride home, April turned the radio down and started talking. She was calm and sobering up. She started crying. Not loud cries, just tears falling from her eyes. She kept wiping her face, but I couldn't hear her cry. I was so confused. She honestly was a nice girl. I didn't know how to talk to her. What was I going to say?

"I know you had sex with Adonis. I knew about y'all for a long time. At first I turned a blind eye because I loved him, and we had a family. Then he got crazy. It wasn't just you. There were other girls too. Was I really that terrible? My fiancé was so unsatisfied that not only was he cheating with other women, but he was fucking a man? Do you have any idea how that makes me feel?"

Sometimes there are just no words, and this was one of those times. I wasn't going to throw myself or Adonis under the bus. I just kept my mouth shut. We pulled in front of the house. She wasn't at all happy with my silence.

"Don't worry. If you don't feel it now, you will when you fall in love. It's called Karma asshole! Someone is going to fuck your man and smile in your face. You're going to understand the hurt I feel right now. He was supposed to be my husband Samuel!"

She slammed the door and was gone.

What she said to me touched me, in a way. But, I knew I wasn't falling in love, so it didn't matter. I got what I wanted. That's how I felt. I had nothing to do with the way she satisfied her man. He wanted me, and I wanted him. She was irrelevant.

******

After Adonis, I swore not to let myself get emotionally tied to anyone again. I had business on my mind. I knew it was time to invest in something. One of my escorting clients was a real estate professional. He told me to call him when I was ready to invest. He found me an agent and helped me pay all required fees. By October, I was a homeowner with rental property and residual income. I was out of the game, but I hit him off proper. He had helped me achieve the American dream, so a nut or two wasn't going to hurt. He paid $15,000 to fuck me two months straight at his leisure. Every time he got horny like this, I would take the money and purchase a rental property. He walked me through the entire process. He helped me find a tenant for the rental property and kept my mortgage extremely low compared to the rent. I made money hand over fist.

I went to see Jonathan for my birthday. I was turning 25. I considered that an important milestone. We were going to go out and dance our cares away. 2004 had been a rollercoaster year. Things were on the up-and-up. Jonathan was a mess when I got to his house. He hadn't been shaving. His apartment was a filthy mess. He had taken a leave of absence from work and was sitting around getting fat and living like a slob. I was disgusted. It was my birthday weekend, and he looked like a cave man. He hadn't cleaned in preparation for my visit. On top of that, he didn't even want to go out. I was pissed. He just wanted to lie around the house. I was very agitated. I didn't come from Minneapolis to sit in the house on my birthday weekend. Hell no! He had to get up.

We went to Club Delta in D.C. I had a blast. Jonathan was strange and distant all night. On the way back to his place, I confronted him. I told him he was acting real fucked up by not wanting to go out and then not even really partying with me once we got there. It was my birthday BITCH! He apologized and said he didn't feel safe in his surroundings. He felt that someone might try and do something to him. He said he wasn't involved with anyone strange. I brushed it off as paranoia. I went back to Minneapolis and brought in the New Year with my family. What was 2005 going to bring me? Would I finally have some stability?

Well, there is always one thing you can count on, and that's drama. The New Year was still very new when Aunt Sylvia called to tell me. My best friend Jonathan was at Methodist Hospital in the psych ward. Someone apparently put something in his drink, and he didn't know anyone. I lost it and rushed to Gary to be by my friend's side.

By the time I arrived, I wasn't allowed to see him. It was family only. I saw his mother. She told me the entire story. The doctors didn't know if it was temporary or permanent. They didn't even know what it was that caused him to deteriorate. He didn't either. I prayed that he would get better. I drove back to Minneapolis feeling heartbroken. I didn't want to lose another friend. We had so much living to do.

Jonathan eventually got better. But he was never the same.

CHAPTER FIFTEEN

HE IS THE BEST THING I EVER HAD

After the Adonis debacle, I ran around a lot. The rental properties and work were going well, but I had no luck in the relationship department. I wasn't interested in just having sex. At the time, I didn't know exactly what I wanted. I figured I'd have fun with the wrong guys until the right one came along. Felicia took notice of my behavior right before the 2006 New Year. She sat me down and asked when I was going to settle down. Settling down was exactly what I wanted to do, but all the guys I met were assholes or didn't have anything to bring into a relationship. Hell, they were all DL niggas. I thought of making my New Year's resolution—no sex in 2007. That wasn't going to happen. I didn't know what to tell her. I could see the concern in her face. What was I going to do?

I looked Felicia directly in the eyes and told her I was going to settle down the day I never have to wake up from a dream. The man I wanted didn't exist. He would be an openly gay, masculine man who is true and honest, who would love me, flaws and all. He would be A MAN, not a leech looking for a place to eat, shit and sleep. He would be someone with drive, integrity and determina-

133

tion. He would put me first. I was tired of being second to some-one's "girlfriend" or his "real life" for that matter. I wanted a lot of attention. He would have to be bold and blunt, not to mention mouth-dropping, heart-pounding, and oh my god he's coming this way fine. He cannot be dark-skinned at all. I like caramel or red bone men. I want him to have a muscular build, not too big but like a track star with a moderate amount of body hair.

We shared a nice laugh. Felicia tried to assure me he would come along when the time was right. At that moment, I knew I would be single for the rest of my life. Who was she kidding? When and where would I find a man that incredible?

******

I did want 2007 to be different. In order for it to be different, I needed to find new people to be around, so I made a BGC page. BGC was the Black Gay Chat network or the "Boys and Girls Club". I heard a lot about it, and decided to try it out. I was online for about a month and met a few people. No one really piqued my interest except this boy from Chicago. His picture was delicious. He was absolutely stunning. I could only imagine what he looked like in person. We talked for a little over a month and exchanged numbers. I was hesitant to pursue him because he was 20 years old. His conversation, however, was beyond his years. We could talk about anything. I really felt like I knew him. He said he worked at Methodist Hospital as a janitor and just moved to Minnesota from Chicago with his best friends. They lived in a three-bedroom apart-ment in Hopkins, which was a 20 minute ride from Minneapolis. His name was Price. He was pursuing me hard. I liked being pur-sued. I thought he was fine, and I did want to get to know him. The age gap was a real problem for me. Seven years was a lot of time between us. The few times we spoke were because he called. It was usually the highlight of the day. He paid attention to me, and I liked it.

******

I was promoted to Assistant Manager of a bank in March of 2007. This year was really panning out well. I decided since I had a new title, I needed a new car. Upgrade for an upgrade, you know. I traded in the Pontiac for a midnight blue 2006 Dodge Charger. It was loaded with all my favorite amenities. Cruise control, power windows, power seats and tinted windows. It was sitting on 22-inch rims. I had to show it off. The next evening I went to a friend's for some beers, blunts and a chance to shine. We opened a six-pack of Coronas and realized we were out of blunt wraps. I wanted to show off.

He lived on the wrong side of the one way. You had to make a right, and there were no U-turns at the light. I was high and was not about to drive up two lights to drive back three, so I jumped across three lanes and flipped the "U." My back tires weren't in the same lane as the front tires, before a cop pulled me over. Damn! I looked around and realized the beer bottle was with me, open. I tried to distract the officer when he came to the window, but he noticed the open Corona. He mentioned he could arrest me before he left with my driver's license and insurance card.

I was high and wigging out. Totally hysterical! My phone rang, and I was happy. I needed someone to talk to. When I realized it was Price, I was even more relieved. I told him about the ridiculousness I was sitting in the middle of, and he told me to calm down. He said to explain to the officer I was making a store run for a friend. He told me to tell the officer I didn't realize I had gotten in the car with the bottle. He then told me to call him back. The officer came back to the car, and I gave the story Price coached me on. I even told him to look, and he would see that I hadn't even touched it. He believed me and let me go with citations for an open bottle ticket and illegal U-turn. I was so happy I had gotten away with just a ticket. I called Price. I wanted to thank him for his help. I asked if he wanted to meet up, chill and smoke. I could hear him smiling through the phone. I was too. He gave me the address. I was on my way.

I called when I was pulling up to the apartment to tell him to come outside. I got stuck on my thought when I pulled into the buildings round-about and saw this very handsome boy on the steps. He had the deepest waves I'd ever seen. They were like a jet-black ocean. He had a caramel complexion, full lips, and his attire was right. I heard Price say hello. I blurted, "Hey, I'm pulling up. Is this you on the steps?" He said no. I felt a little embarrassed and disappointed too. That other boy was fine. Price said he was coming and hung up. Just then, the boy on the steps started walking towards my car. I had the windows tinted, so I stared hard. He was sagging, had a slight bowleg and his skin looked like it was glowing under the sun. It looked soft and supple, like a warm towel right out of a dryer filled with Downy fabric softener sheets. He had to be at least 150 pounds solid. I rolled the window down and got lost in his hazel eyes. He asked what was up and introduced himself as Price. It seemed as if there were a million mini-me's jumping around and dancing inside me. He was absolutely gorgeous. Everything I was looking for. I smiled and without hesitation told him to get in the car.

We were going to my house. We first stopped to get some smoke and wraps. We talked about a lot during the 20-minute ride. He explained he was working at the hospital but had plans and needed something better. He wanted to take care of his family and was searching for a job that would allow him to do that. His presence was strong. He was manly. I welcomed it. He sat as close to me in the car as he could and had his hand on my thigh the entire ride. He was so attentive it scared me. I wasn't used to that behavior. I always wanted public intimacy.

We made it to my house, rolled a blunt and talked even more. Someone was calling his phone repeatedly. He never answered. I didn't pay attention to it. I was flattered actually. He put the phone to the side and gave me his undivided attention. I loved the way he looked at me. It was like he could see ME—the deep dark part of me—but he didn't care. He wanted to be right beside me. I wanted that too. I felt like I could tell him my secrets and deepest desires without being judged. I lay across his lap while we smoked the blunt, ate popcorn and watched TV. I told him I really wanted a man. Someone who'd hold my hand in public; someone I could hold and kiss and love, whenever and wherever I wanted. I had a mouth full of popcorn when Price turned my head and swept me away into his hazel brown eyes, "I want to hold your hand and kiss you in public. I don't care what anyone else says about how or when I show my affection."

I smiled. My heart was flying. I knew at that moment that Price was my soul mate. "You're going to be my husband one day!"

We both smiled. He moved closer to my face and softly pecked my lips. I went back for more. More was exactly what I got.

We had the most amazing experience. Price was sensually-aggressive. He freaked me in every way imaginable. The way he fit inside of me and held me was unbelievable. I came two times back to back without even touching myself. I was in love. I'd been looking for that feeling since the first time I was with Coop. This time was different. This man was gay, all the way GAY. He was making me feel like no straight man ever had. He stole my heart and then ravaged my body. There was no wonder why he never went home.

I had so many relationships that went nowhere. They were dead-ends from the beginning. They were just flings. I was never in love, nor did I feel loved while I was with any of them. Price took me somewhere I had never been. He showed me he was truly for me. He was my dream. I never had to wake up.

******

Soon Price and I were inseparable. We were together every single day just loving each other. We finished each other's sentences; reached over each other for the remote; shared the toothpaste and made dinner together. I got off work at night, but the sun was always shinning in my house. I went home to love, good, hard, strong love. I truly had met my soul mate. I was happy. By Easter, I was introducing him to the family. We went to Felicia's first. I knew her house would be fun. I wanted to get "right" before I went to visit everyone else. Felicia loved Price. She found him just as intriguing as I did. Grandma Hazel was at Aunt Teresa's, along with my other cousins. They were so receptive. I was amazed. My grandmother brought tears to my eyes when she told Price that she would love to see more of him. That meant the world to me. My grandmother accepted us as one.

Around Memorial Day weekend, we drove to Gary, Indiana, to see my father. I wanted to introduce Price to my father and stepmom, Frieda, but I was nervous. I never had a direct conversation with my father about my sexuality. Now I was standing in his house introducing him to my boyfriend. I felt like I could tell Frieda anything, so I started with her. She embraced Price and told me not to be nervous. She assured me my father was not a judgmental man. When he came home, I was extra nervous, scared and sweating. All I could think of was rejection. I couldn't stop staring at my father while we were talking. I was trying to gauge his attitude and see what his mood was like. Every thought in the world was running through my mind. I couldn't stop thinking of how far we'd come, and how I didn't want this to turn us around. I thought about every conversation we'd had. Then I began to think of my mother and how she responded when I first came out. I was a mess.

We were sitting on the sofa, when I decided I didn't want to tell my father. He got up to get something to drink from the kitchen. The looks he delivered to Price and me completely sent me over the edge. I got scared and told Frieda now wasn't a good time. I wasn't going to tell him. She assured me everything would be alright. She would tell him if I wanted her to. That seemed a little easier. I agreed to it. She asked me if I was sure. I said, yes. He returned to his chair, directly across from Price and me, and asked me, what's going on?

I laughed nervously and asked what he was talking about. He looked at me and said, "I know you by now son. Something is on your mind. I want to know what you're thinking."

Before I could say anything Frieda interjected, "Baby, Sam has something he wants to tell you."

"I know that. That's why I asked. What's going on?"

She said while glaring at him, "Okay, baby, this is Price and Sam."

"Really? Well I didn't know that!" She delivered another sideways glare.

"Okay let me put it another way. Baby, this is Sam's boyfriend, Price. Price this is Sam's father, Samuel."

My father looked at Price. "Is this a joke?"

It was my turn to bat. "No. This is my boyfriend. We live together in Minneapolis. We love each other."

My father then placed his hands over his face and was quiet a minute.

"Are you okay?" I didn't know what else to say. He asked me to give him a minute to gather himself. I was nervous as hell. He got up out of his seat and walked over to Price.

"Price, give me a hug."

I was so relieved. My father and Price hugged. Then my father gave me a hug. "As long as you're happy, I'm happy for you. You are my son. I am going to love you regardless. Is this what you have been keeping from me?"

I told him it was, and he told me to never keep anything from him again. We enjoyed the rest of the weekend. I was on a cloud the entire time. I had a man who grab my hand and kiss me in the middle of a grocery store, and my family accepted him. I was in a place I had never seen before. I was in the state of Pure Happiness.

✶✶✶✶✶✶

Price was the one. I woke up on cloud nine every morning. Most mornings I didn't want to get up because I didn't want to leave his side. I had given my all in many relationships. I had given my time, energy and emotion all to no avail. I thanked GOD for bringing Price into my life. I thanked Price for accepting me entirely. He loved me so hard. It was like I really was dreaming. No one had ever had that type of power over me. I was following his lead, and I liked it. He would always say, "Bae, in the end, it's only you and me." I was just fine with that Price and I talked about any and everything, we kept no secrets, it was bliss.

We planned to take a week-long trip to Orlando, Florida, with Jonathan, in June. I was excited. This would be our first real vacation together, and he was meeting one of my best friends. A few days before the trip, Price was acting odd. I didn't want to seem insecure, so I didn't say anything to him directly. Instead, I decided to go through his wallet. They always say, "Don't go looking for what you don't want to find." True to the saying, what I found really pissed me off. I found a condom, two numbers and an email address. So I did what any person would do that's in love. I set it up to know if he was using the condoms. I placed a small line of ink on the corner of the wrapper of the condom; programmed one of the numbers belonging to a Luciano in my phone and wrote the other one down to call later.

The next day he was pulled over. The tint on the car windows was "too dark." The car was impounded because he didn't have a license. I was annoyed with him. I planned to spend the weekend packing and getting things in order for our trip, but Price had other plans. He told me he was going to the club with his friends. He didn't invite me, and I wasn't really in the mood to go out. I stayed home.

Around 4:30 am, I rolled over and Price was not beside me. I saw his clothes on the floor and could hear snoring coming from the living room. He was home. I found him knocked out on the floor. He was sleeping hard, like he did after we had sex, slobbering and snoring. He was naked on the floor, and it turned me on. I tried to wake him up to let him know t I wanted to have sex. He was in a deep sleep. He didn't even budge. I was seething with anger. Seemed someone else had put my man to bed. I began the search through his things. I started with his cell phone, three recent numbers. Two of which I recognized from the wallet. The newest one was placed at 2:15 am after the club let out.

I immediately started looking for the wallet. I found it in the back pocket of his shorts. The condom was gone. The wrapper was in the front pocket of his pants. It was the exact same wrapper with the little ink line. I was furious. What was the meaning of this? I thought we were happy. I felt hurt, disappointed, betrayed, used and abused all over again. I'd done a lot for Price. I had invested more of myself than I'd ever invested in anyone. He met my family and lived in my house. He wasn't working and drove my car whenever he wanted, without a license, and he cheated on me. I put on my Timberland boots, went to the living room and kicked him as hard as I could. Price jumped up startled and confused.

"Why the hell did you just kick me?"

I was standing with the empty condom wrapper in my hand, "What the hell is this bitch?"

His eyes widened. He looked like a deer caught in someone's headlights. "It's not what you're thinking, Sam! My boy used it."

"And gave you back the empty wrapper? You must take me as a damn fool Price!"

He laid back down and went to sleep as if nothing happened. I started to kick him again, but decided it was best that I didn't. I didn't want to hurt him.

I went back in the room and cried. What had he done? Why? Everything was going so well. Four months of magic and now this. Someone was trying to wake me up from my dream. I didn't like that at all. I woke up the next morning puffy-eyed with a headache. Price was sitting on the couch smoking a cigarette and watching TV. I sat beside him and asked what he did with the condom. He concocted some insane story about not wanting to hurt my feelings last night and not wanting to tell me the truth. I wasn't masculine enough for him at times. I was heartbroken all over again. He continued admitting he didn't go to the club and instead hung out with his straight friends. They were smoking and drinking. After he dropped everyone off, he was so horny he masturbated in the car and used the condom to catch his cum. What an amazing story. I knew deep down in my heart that he was lying, but I loved him. He said he loved me. I let it go. I carried on like nothing ever happened.

Thursday we left for Florida, and I felt this trip was exactly what we needed. There was some hostility in the house because of Price's carelessness. We needed to get away. Price had never been on an airplane. He was excited and nervous. We took off holding hands and looking into each other's eyes to a whole new level. His eyes used to put me in a trance. I thought I was flying right to heaven with my king. After awhile, Price started looking out the window. He was like a child. He was amazed at how small everything got as we got higher. We shared headphones and listened to the radio. I fell asleep, and before long we were in sunny Florida.

As we got off the plane, my best friend was waiting for us. Jonathan's plane arrived fifteen minutes before ours. I introduced Price and Jonathan. They began to have some difference of opinions right away. I tried to keep the air cool and took pictures while we waited for the shuttle bus to take us to get a rental car. I was happy. None of the cares or worries of the past week were with me. It was just my best friend and my lover at my side.

Jonathan was doing a lot better. He was somewhat himself. Nothing compared to how he was before his incident. We got the rental car and headed to the resort. Price and Jonathan kept going at each other. I felt as if I were playing a game of tug-of-war between them. They were cool one minute and at each other's throat the next. I could tell Jonathan was upset when we were checking into the resort. He wanted to go to the club later. Price wasn't 21, so that wasn't really an option. When we got to the room, Jonathan continued to antagonize Price. While I was lying across his lap Jonathan threw a piece of paper at Price and yelled, "that's for you little boy!" When he read, "Kids eat free!" Price blew up. I started laughing. I could not hold it. I really tried. I could tell Price was very offended. So I told Jonathan to cool down. We didn't come here for this; we're going to have fun.

Our first day there, we drove to Daytona Beach to hang out with my cousin Sharee. We got lost going to Daytona Beach, and Price and Jonathan were at it again. I just ignored them and focused on the road. Sharee was excited when we arrived. I hadn't seen her in a long time and was happy someone else was around to help me ignore the boys. She showed us around town. We rode up and down the strips and watched as a space shuttle launched from Kennedy Space Center. It was a beautiful experience.

Our final day in Florida was by far one of the best days of my life. Price knew I was afraid of water. He knew, no matter what, I was not getting anywhere near the water. So he purchased me a float in an attempt to lure me into the pool. Price, Jonathan, and Sharee were swimming and playing as I sat to the side and watched. It was so hot that day. I wanted so badly to get in, but that wasn't going to happen. Price wasn't interested in my excuses. He was in the pool and wanted me in the water as well. He walked over to me, dripping freezing cold water, and promised me he had my back and wouldn't let me fall into the water. His tone took all my fears away. I trusted him. He wouldn't let me drown. Before long, I was on that float. I was screaming and trying to hold onto him. He was smiling and spinning me around. I was scared as hell, but it was so much fun.

Everyone at the pool was looking, including the kids. Price didn't care at all. He just kept being him. He leaned in and kissed me. I swore the earth moved. I saw nothing but stars when I closed my eyes. The pool was getting a little crowded. People started throwing shade, so we went to the beach where we played in the water for hours like we were all little kids again. By night's fall, we were exhausted. We dropped Sharee off and returned to the room. The night was calm and peaceful. Price wanted to walk on the beach, and I was all for it. We took a long walk together and talked as we held hands. He walked behind me and held my waist, kissed me, and we gazed into the night looking at the stars. That night Price wanted to fall asleep in my arms. It was strange because I'd never held anyone before. I knew sometimes we all needed a hug, and if my guy wanted to be held then I would hold him.

******

My dream was purposely being invaded by nasty happiness thieves. I didn't want to believe anything bad was happening, but the evidence was piling up. By late July, all kinds of suspicious activities were occurring. I was at my wits end. I was washing his clothes and found shit stains in the front of his boxers. Painting Picasso was unacceptable. I had no choice but to put him out. Shit stains in the front could only mean one thing. We had sex at home and showered after each time. Where could they have come from? I didn't even bother trying to get a story out of him. I simply put him out. August 1, 2007, I was single again. Price was back in Chicago. I was devastated. How could this happen? We were amazing. Perfect. I did everything he wanted. I allowed my heart to open and receive him, and now he had broken it.

Moving on was difficult. I was so thankful for Felicia, who was truly my best friend. She was the kind of shoulder you knew would be there no matter what. She never judged me and always knew exactly what to say. She gave the best advice during that period. Number one, relationships with your friends are give and take. We shouldn't choose friends or want friends and relationships that don't do anything for us besides take from us and pull us down. My only problem was I didn't think Price was pulling me down. I wanted him. I was hoping he was thinking about me, as much as I was thinking of him. We had not been apart since the first day we were together. I was so alone without him. No one could love me like that, and I wanted it back. I wanted that feeling back.

Meanwhile, work was keeping me busy. I was on the market for another rental property. Rental income was easy money. It was far easier than escorting. I wanted to get as deep into that market as I could. I found another home in October, and with two rental homes and a job, I was in the money all over again.

Four months have passed and Price and I were still not together. He called on my birthday, I was so happy, but I wanted to move a little slower. I made many trips to Chicago to see him. I was still in love. I couldn't let him go. He found another job and from what I could see was doing what he needed to. Finally, in March 2008, he came back home. We spent the entire month wrapped in each other. I missed him so much. By April we wanted something that belonged to both of us, so we moved into a two-bedroom town house and got a cat. The townhouse was cute, perfect for the two of us and the cat. It was a Tabby breed cat. That's what we named hi, "Tabby." He was so cute with a dust orange color and white accents, he was very affectionate. Tabby was our child. Everything was perfect again. There was talk of a gay marriage ban debate on news channels all over the TV. I, of course, was tuned in every night to see what was going to happen. I wasn't necessarily thinking about getting married. I wanted to know what my options were if the opportunity presented itself. I was watching the news and making dinner when Price asked me the most shocking question.

"What would you say if I said I wanted to spend the rest of my life with you? What would you say Sam?"

I could have passed out right then and there. Was he serious? What would I say? "I would love to spend the rest of my life with you."

I couldn't believe what I was hearing. I was completely unprepared for this. There was chicken in the stove, and Tabby's liter box needed to be cleaned. "Are you fucking kidding me? OF COURSE I WILL MARRY YOU!"

Just like that, May became a month to remember. We started making the arrangements and prepared to pick a date.

******

While at her daughter's house on July 11, 2008, Aunt Theresa had a heart attack. Kiwana tried to perform CPR, but it didn't work. I was in the midst of planning a wedding, and one of my close aunts passed away. I was devastated. She had a beautiful ceremony at Redeemer Missionary Baptist Church and a repast at Felicia's. The entire scene was sad. Aunt Theresa was the one who held the family together after Uncle Kenny passed away. Now what was going to happen?

CHAPTER SIXTEEN

YOU AND ME: VOWS

W^e were getting married on August 4, 2008, the day after Price's 22nd birthday. The ceremony was going to take place in California. The state was all over the news because they were going to lift the ban on same-sex marriages again, and we wanted to be a part of history. I was so excited! I sent out 150 invitations for our reception ceremony, which would take place in Minneapolis, on August 23, on a "196 foot yacht!" We were going to sail up the Mississippi River while having dinner, dancing and listening to good music. I was getting married. I wanted the best.

San Francisco, California! We arrived on Friday, August 1st, with the intention on having a great pre-wedding weekend. Price's friend was acting as our witness and met us at the airport. We were staying on the 17th floor of the Intercontinental Hotel, in downtown San Francisco. The hotel was brand new. We could have very well been the first people to stay in our room. I couldn't believe this was really happening. I was in California to marry the man I loved. You know my cycle. The good has to come with something bad. When Price got a "toothache" after we landed, I wasn't surprised.

He was in excruciating pain. He cried and wanted to stay in the room in bed the entire weekend. I couldn't let a toothache and a crying 21 year old ruin the most important weekend of my life. I went shopping.

Price decided doping himself with pain pills would be the best course of action and was snoring sleep when I returned to the room. I was happy and hoped the next day the pain would be gone, and he would be in better spirits. We were getting married in two days. This was a time of excitement and celebration. When I got up the next morning and found Price still in the same miserable mood, I called his mom. I knew that a mother's love could take away any pain. It was the day before his birthday. We were in sunny California. I needed his focus to get right. Right on time, birthday morning Price's pain was gone. I believe the call to his mom did the trick. We did some shopping, went to dinner, and spent our last night together as a couple. Early Monday morning we went to City Hall and exchanged vows. He placed the one karat, princess cut, white gold, diamond band on my finger. I could never express the tremendous amount of emotion I was experiencing. He told us we could kiss. We were now "Husband and Husband." Price wasn't my friend, someone I was having sex with or even a boyfriend. He was my husband. I was now Mr. Price Hilton. It felt amazing.

We went to dinner and retired to the room. He wasn't my husband 24 hours before we had an argument about sex. The mood of the day was completely ruined. We didn't consummate our marriage. In fact we just smoked and drank wine until we fell asleep. We returned to Minneapolis the next morning not speaking. I couldn't understand why my husband didn't want to make love to me. He didn't understand why I was mad. We both kept attitudes and went about our business. A marriage made in heaven.

I checked on my tenants when I got back. I had four properties now. Everyone was fine. I performed regular maintenance on the homes, and they were taken care of. Work was the same. At this point, I was an Assistant Manager. I worked set hours and knew what my paycheck was all the time. Professionally, I was a gold star. At home, on the other hand, it was not the dream I was I praying for, but we had to keep moving forward. I went on with the reception as planned. Family and friends came from all over. I even paid for hotel stays, to ensure certain people would be able to come. It was beautiful. We wore white and green tuxedos and crisp white Air Force One Sneakers. We were speaking again. We finally consummated our marriage, so the mood was magic. Everyone was happy, and the fun was contagious. We partied up the Mississippi River on "a 196-foot yacht" and back down with our 144 guests from 6 o'clock pm until 10 o'clock pm. It was an amazing time!

******

Back in the reality realm there was work, work, work and more work. I was the sole financial provider. We never wanted for anything at all. Price couldn't keep a job, and when he had one he spent all of his money on electronics and other frivolous things. He had a good life. I was happy and wanted to make sure my husband was smiling too.

We went to Hawaii for a week in December. We were celebrating two things, our honeymoon and my birthday. We were right on the beach. I could smell the salt water when the wind blew. I loved it. It was completely different from when I first visited. The mood was different. When I was with Jonathan, I was single and just there to be there. Price was my husband. We were doing married tourist things together. We went to a luau and saw a whole pig roasted and served over a fire. We took a tour of Pearl Harbor and other historic sites. We rode around the city on mopeds, shopped and went to the beach and we lived it up. I was in love with my husband, and in heaven.

******

Price's aunt fell on hard times in Chicago and didn't have anywhere to live. He offered her our spare room. We drove to Chicago to get her and her son and decided we might as well spend the holiday there with his family. It wasn't a bad thing. I didn't celebrate holiday's heavy, so it was something new. I loved my in-laws and got along with them. We always had fun together. After Christmas, we loaded the car with his aunt's things, her, and her son, and we headed back to Minneapolis.

We brought in the New Year at the the "Gay 90s" club. Shabastion didn't care for Price, so we didn't really chill anymore. The club was packed. We needed some breathing space.

The Disco Room was partly empty, so we stood in there for a moment. Price was high and feeling really loose and relaxed. He started *voguing?!* I was taken aback. Voguing was a feminine thing. He was masculine. I felt lied to, but the confidence he projected while he did it turned me on. We partied the rest of the night and had an amazing time, but I couldn't get the image of Price voguing out of my head. I figured he had to have been a bottom before. I wanted clarification, so I asked him. He told me he had indeed "bottomed" for someone before. He didn't like it, so he didn't do it again. I was mad. What could I do? I had been a top for someone before. I guess we have to see what we don't like to be certain about what it is we do like.

2009 started with a bang. One day, Price picked me up from work, I just wanted to unwind and relax. I got in the passenger seat and started to change the CD to Keisha Cole when he flipped out and started screaming. Apparently, I was too flamboyant for my husband. This was the man who once said he would hold my hand, kiss me in public whenever and wherever. He started taking all of my female R&B CD's and throwing them out of the car window. I was stunned. I didn't know what had come over him. I wanted to punch him in the head. I was furious. He hadn't paid for any of those CD's. He was just throwing them out the window. I'm too feminine and flamboyant? It took him almost two years and a $25,000 wedding, $10,000 cleaning his credit and $1,100 getting his driver's license reinstated to figure that out. I wanted to get home and get out of the car. I didn't have time to deal with his childish behavior and immaturity. I had a long day at work. He was about to release a side of me I had buried years ago. I went in the house, showered and went to bed. I was not in any way going to entertain him.

******

The next day at work I learned that my boss was promoted and leaving our branch. That meant her position was going to open. I was always about my money, so I applied for the job. They always consider in-house candidates first. I got an interview immediately. I was so excited I called the house to tell Price, but there was no answer. A few hours later, while I was on a conference call at work, I received a call on my cell from Price telling me the townhouse had burnt down. What the hell did he do? I later learned from the leasing office that the maintenance installed a faulty furnace, and it caused our home to burn down within 30 minutes. It was a total loss.

I was cussing and going crazy on my cell in disbelief. Suddenly, I heard another voice say, "Samuel". I realized I hadn't put the office phone on mute. The other managers heard everything I was saying. I apologized and told them I had to go. I grabbed my keys and ran out the front door of the bank. The entire ride home I was wondering what I was going home to. I found out when I pulled up. There was nothing—nothing at all. Everything was gone except for a few clothing items and pictures. Tabby survived, and that was a relief. Price's aunt's things were gone too. I was so sad. Everything was either burned, had smoke damage or damaged by water. Thank God for renters insurance. At least I knew we were covered.

My boss called me that night and told me I didn't have to go to the interview in the morning. It was rescheduled due to my disaster. It was a nice gesture, but I wasn't going to let this slow me down. This was my cycle; something good always brought something bad. I was not playing into it. I wanted a promotion. I deserved it. I knew I could run the branch. I told her I would be there tomorrow, bright-eyed and bushy tailed ready for my interview. But I needed to know if it would be alright to wear jeans. My boss laughed and said sure, and there was no need to say anymore.

Price and I compiled a list of everything we lost, down to the Q-tips. Then we went to the 24-hour Walmart and got the necessities. We were staying in a hotel, courtesy of our insurance. Price and I cried and held each other all night. He consoled me. I consoled him. We were about to start over. I had to know he was still with me. A lot of chaos was floating around us. I wanted it all to stop. I fell asleep in my husband's arms.

The next morning I was a mess. I had to be in Wisconsin at 10 am for my interview. It was about a 30-minute ride. I wanted to make sure I was gone early in case of traffic. We kissed goodbye, and I was on the road. The interview lasted over an hour. They took notice and asked me about my attire, "Why did you still come rather than wait until you had the proper dress?"

The answer was simple and straight to the point. "The bank was still open," I answered. "The branch had to be run, and I lead by example."

We weren't in the hotel four days before Price started being irate and obnoxious again. We were in a double suite because his aunt was still living with us. Apparently, she wasn't keeping the room as immaculate as Price liked, so he turned into the Incredible Hulk. When I got home from work, he had her bags at the door ready to put them in the car. He put his own aunt out when she was four months pregnant with her second child. She told me she was not going to be controlled by a broke fag and would rather be in Chicago where she knew other people and didn't have to deal with Price's mood swings. She and her son got in the car. Price took them to the bus station.

I was promoted to Branch Manager effective February 1, 2009 and the same week we moved into another town house in the same complex. Nothing could seem to work in a peaceful flow. Price was jealous of me because I was making a nice amount of money between my job and four tenants. He would often make crude remarks about me thinking I was the shit because I was a manager. If I didn't have my job or the houses, I wouldn't be anything. I thought we were supposed to be a team. I didn't keep anything from him. He had access to everything. How did he think he ate at night? Not because he was purchasing groceries, toilet paper, or laundry detergent for that matter. I got Price four different jobs; he quit all of them. Was that my fault? I paid for him to get his GED. He still had not taken the test. I couldn't deal with him.

******

My house was not a home. No matter how hard I tried, Price was not satisfied. We got the insurance check in March, almost two months later. He tried to take it and spend it all. Once again, he was in the store with a millionaire budget and no job. I stressed for him to get only what we needed—a couch, TV, beds, and nothing more. He didn't like the way I was overseeing the money. I worked hard, and it was my money. I was going to say whatever I felt needed to be said. The relationship was so distant and foreign. I didn't know the man I lived with and was married to. I didn't know what to do.

I thought if we went to Chicago for the Fourth of July holiday, maybe Price would get out of his negative rut. We weren't having sex; we were arguing all the time; I just was not smiling like I used to. It didn't work. It was like he was on his cycle or going through menopause or something. He was hot and cold. Being around him was not as pleasant as it once was. I wanted to figure out why? I took a "week's vacation" in the middle of the month, so we could spend time together and rekindle our romance. I was married. I was not going to let it fall apart under me and not know why. I was there with him in the mornings and sleeping in late with him just like we used to. Price's phone, however, was getting a suspicious amount of unavailable calls. They started every day around 10am for two mornings. The look on his face every time that call came through let me know something was up. He never answered the phone and kept saying someone was playing on his phone.

It didn't make sense to keep letting the phone ring. He needed to pick it up and see who it was. It could have been a wrong number. The caller could stop wasting his time. The phone rang again. I decided to answer. There was a boy on the other end. I asked who he was trying to reach. He said Price, loud and clear. He was sitting right beside me, but I wasn't going to hand him the phone.

"Once again, who is this" I asked? "How do you know Price?" I needed answers, and I need them ASAP!

"Aren't you supposed to be at work?"

I was in total disbelief. Did this stranger just check me? Asking why I wasn't at work. How did he know I was even supposed to be at work? "WHO ... THE FUCK ... IS THIS?" I was getting irritated. I think the boy finally picked up on it.

"Well, I met Price on the chat line. He came over my house. I stay on the North side. Anyway, I'm pissed he just stopped answering my calls. I'm not the person you hit and quit. I will not be had like that."

I was speechless. He continued. "Price told me about you. You work at a bank or something five days a week, Monday-Friday, off Tuesdays, same hours every day. You're his husband. I mean, I don't have anything to do with that. I was supposed to come over, but like I said he hasn't been answering. I guess I know why now. You're home."

My blood was boiling. All I needed to know now was if they had sex. I asked, and he said no, but we have given each other head. You gave each other WHAT?

I threw the phone hard, aiming at Price's head, and left the house. Once again, he fucked over on me. He followed me outside and swore the guy was lying. Lying? This stranger knew things about me he shouldn't have known, and I was to believe that everything else he said was false. We didn't have sex the entire month of July nor was he showing me any affection. Anytime I tried to show him some, he'd start an argument to ensure I was out of the mood. There wasn't even make-up sex. We used to have sex all the time, and now we weren't. Some boy was just on his phone running my schedule down to me. The signs were all over the place but again, I stayed. I loved him. He was my everything. He was my husband. What was I to do? Just leave him?

If we weren't arguing over sex, it was because I had lit the blunt from the wrong end, or it was burning wrong, or the chicken was dry, or the toilet seat was up. Hell, anything could start an altercation. I told him he purposely picked arguments, so he would have a reason to leave the house. He ignored me and left the house. I was over so much. I felt like I was calling his mother, aunt or Felicia every day. This was not the dream I wanted. This was not the man I met. Price changed so much. I didn't know what was going on with him.

******

In August, we moved into one of my rental units. Our anniversary fell on a Tuesday. I figured we would celebrate at home together, and the following weekend we could have a party. August 4, 2009 made me want to die. I'd given two years to this man, a year of which I was completely committed and devoted to him, and he wanted to argue. It was our anniversary and he wanted to be mad. I just kept to myself. On Friday, his mother, aunt, cousins and a few other relatives came to the house from Chicago. They were staying with us, so they could attend the anniversary party. My temperamental husband was happy again. Things were on the up and up once again. We were happy, affectionate and intimate. We kept his aunt's son and my nieces after the party was over. We had the house. Price was home, so we thought it would be fun to keep them for the rest of the next three weeks. The kids brought a fun and energetic atmosphere to the house. I loved knowing they were home when I got there because they were always smiling, and Price couldn't start stupid arguments. We loved having the kids around and thought we would be excellent parents. We started looking into adoption.

Work was going smoothly. It was just taking up the majority of my week and days. Finally, my husband and I were getting along. I was *Googling* adoption every time I was near a computer. I was excited all over again. We were going to have a family. I was going to be responsible for someone's life. I'd be an amazing parent. I already was. My nieces were like my children. Work was good. I was down to one tenant, but the money was still coming. I was still living how I wanted. By October, the Charger was getting old. I was ready for a new car. On my day off, while Price was at one of his fly by night jobs, I traded it in and got a white 2009 Mitsubishi Gallant. I loved it. I deserved a new car. It was brand new off the assembly line with zero miles just waiting for me to own it. Price didn't like the car. He couldn't afford one, so I didn't care. My money bought my car. If he wanted to be an asshole, I could too.

Price wasn't going to fold easy. He tried to take the car out on several occasions. First in September it was "side-swiped" by a city bus. The mirror was knocked off and paint was scratched. My brand new car, not even a month old, was in the shop already. He got it fixed, well the insurance did, and when he brought it home there were thick black racing strips from the hood across the roof and on the trunk. What the fuck? Now I had a white Mitsubishi with black racing strips. I wanted a low key car. I was a professional. I didn't like the looks and stereotypes I got driving souped-up cars. Price was young. He couldn't understand. I didn't even try to explain it. I just went to work and kept thinking about the baby that would soon be in our home. We were on good terms, and I didn't want to argue with him.

We spent New Year's in Chicago. We had to keep moving or some kind of evil would creep into our home and tear us apart. We took Price's friend Tony with us. We arrived in Chicago a little before midnight and all of a sudden Price had a headache. Tony and I went to Gary and brought in the New Year with my friends. We drove back to Chicago around 3am and Price was gone out with his friends. I guess the headache passed. When he returned, he sat in the living room with Tony and was telling him where he was. I could hear him from the other room telling Tony he was at a bathhouse with his friends. He said he saw all kinds of things, but he didn't do anything. I didn't believe that for a minute. I stormed out the room and asked him if he was fucking serious? He didn't even acknowledge me. He walked directly past me and went into the room. He lay in the bed and fell asleep. I had to be realistic with myself. This relationship, this marriage, was not healthy. I knew it and didn't want to accept it. I knew that we probably wouldn't be together much longer, let alone forever. I couldn't let go. I had to make my marriage work. I didn't want to be another statistic.

******

We started taking adoption classes during the second week of January 2010. It was part of the process. I was still interested in adoption, so I made sure we took them. I was so engulfed in my personal life that my professional life started to fall apart, and I didn't even notice. I was "Branch Manager" for a year, but I wanted to quit. The job wasn't hard, $60,000 a year plus quarterly bonuses.

I got a $7,000 bonus the second quarter I was manager. I was overworked and stressed. We were open seven days a week and short staffed. I was there seven days a week. The job just consumed my life. Price and I were not on good terms, and I wanted to make home happy again. I had to wait a couple of weeks to qualify for my 401K and employee match. Once I did, I was going to quit my job.

I told Price what I was thinking. He was my husband. He should know. Somewhere during the conversation we started talking about moving. It was an extremely cold winter, and we both were sick of the cold weather. Price had convinced me my family and friends didn't like him. We decided to move. I had divulged too much information to my family. I told them negative things that would make anyone who loved you, hate the person you were talking about, and I didn't want anyone to hate Price.

******

I quit my job at the end of February, and started advertising for a tenant so we could rent the house. We looked at the map and decided Dallas, Texas was where we were going to move. It was the only state not hit hard by the recession. I knew finding a job would be easy. The plan was for us to move. Price would get a job, and I would work on my book.

We went through a company called "Pro Move" to find places in Dallas. We rented a car, drove to Chicago, picked up Price's mother, and took a road trip to Dallas. We were just visiting, going to see the different places in person and making all the final decisions pertaining to the move. The weekend went smoothly. We looked at the places and decided on one. I liked the warm weather, and I was ready for a change. This move was going to be a big move. The evil crawled back into Price the night before we left. That morning he was very nasty. His mother looked at him and asked,

"What the fuck is your problem? Why are you acting like a bitch?" He ignored her. She looked at me, apologized, and said, "He got that from his father's side. I'm really sorry."

I tried to ignore the negativity and keep the good spirits. Once we got on the road, Price's mood became more pleasant. We enjoyed the trip back to Minnesota, got our stuff and moved!

******

We moved to Dallas, Texas April 1, 2010. I couldn't have been more excited. Price was smiling. That made me smile. We were moving to a new city, with new people. It was our new beginning. Everything was on the up and up. There were just the two of us and Tabby. Cabin fever was starting to kick in We made the decision to go on BGC and find some friends in Dallas. It was time to get out and discover our new surroundings.

Samar was cute from what I could see on BGC. He was a red bone with a regular build, tattoos, and a nice smile. I hit him up. He said he was cool with being our "Dallas tour guide." We planned to meet Friday, April 16th, go to a local club or bar, and chill. I took my hair down earlier that day and washed it when Price told me he was going to meet Samar. He was talking to him on BGC and thought maybe it was best if he met him first before we went out with him. To make things even more suspicious, Price deleted all of the messages before I could read them. I didn't know what they were about to do.

He left home around 3:30pm. He called home when he got there. He said he was going to come back and get me. When I woke up a little after three in the morning, Price was not home. I had no missed calls. We were in a new state. We didn't know anyone. My husband went to meet a stranger hadn't come home yet, and to make matters worse, he wasn't answering his phone. I began to think the worst. Anything could have happened. It was almost four in the morning. I called my mother-in-law and LaShenia because I didn't know what to do.

His mom said she spoke to him earlier. That was around 11pm. LaShenia said call the police. After I hung up with my sister, I thought about it. I knew in my heart what Price was doing. I still called the police to report him missing. I would rather think he was hurt in the hospital or dead, than to think he was blatantly disrespecting me and our new home. Unfortunately, someone has to be missing for 24-hours before they would take a report. I called LaShenia back with Price's mom on three-way. If it wasn't for them, I wouldn't have made it. Price's mother three-wayed him. The phone rang to the voicemail. She was leaving a voicemail when Price called her back. She told him to call me, and we got off the phone.

His story was impossible, "Hey, I took a Xanax pill and drank a Four Loco. I'm a little too inebriated to drive home."

Well, isn't that what spouses are for? I thought. "What's the address?" I asked.

"I'll take a cab and come to you. You don't know those people. Someone might try to take advantage of you." If the thought of him cheating didn't hurt enough, his reply did.

"I'm not going to do nothing I don't want to do." I was pissed off.

"You know what Price, bring me my damn car!"

"Didn't I just tell you I can't drive? Are you listening? When I gather myself, I'll be home?

"No! What the fuck are you talking about? That is not okay. Give me the address. I'll come get you!

"I'll be home, Sam."

And just like that the phone went dead.

I couldn't believe that he just hung up on me. He was out doing GOD knows what, with GOD knows who, and he had the nerve to have attitude with me. He came in a little after five o'clock. He was a disgusting mess. I tried to talk to him but he couldn't stay awake. I was infuriated, but there was no point trying to talk to him. I walked him to the bedroom and put him in the bed. I lay next to him and cried. I knew he cheated. Here he was in our bed snoring like things were sweet.

Price woke up around two o'clock in the afternoon and B-lined straight into the bathroom to shower. I was sitting on the couch smoking a Newport shaking my leg. I never went to sleep. My mind was so heavy. I was so confused I couldn't even fathom sleeping. I didn't know what to do. I heard the shower turn off and thought of going in there and fighting him while he was wet, but I didn't even have the strength to fight. He went in the room and threw on shorts and a tee and went into the kitchen and started making food. He didn't even acknowledge me. Didn't ask me if I was hungry or wanted anything? He made his food and sat on the couch next to me without a care in the world. We didn't say anything to each other. Before long, he went in the room and got dressed. I heard car keys jingle. I asked him if he was fucking serious. Was he really about to leave with my car? True to Price style he brushed me off, asked me why is everything always mine? We were married? Then told me I should go log into BGC and meet someone and have them come get me and walked out the door. I started crying.

I don't think I've ever smoked a cigarette so hard. I was going crazy. I loved Price, but I wasn't willing to take the shit he was dishing out. That's when Robert kicked in. I was having a full-on conversation with myself trying to figure out what I was going to do. I thought I was truly going crazy. I was going to have a talk with Price that night to tell him I was willing to forgive his indiscretions and work on our marriage as long as he promised never to do it again. Silly I know. If he didn't agree, I was going to move to California and file for divorce. I knew that I deserved better than what he was giving me.

Things were not like they were in the beginning. He asked me to marry him and then completely changed. LaShenia and Felicia knew what was going on and told me I could stay with either one of them if that's what it came to. I knew California was the way to go. I would most definitely be filing for divorce if I left.

******

Price didn't come home Saturday night or Sunday either. I didn't bother to call. I still couldn't sleep. I was not going to continuously call MY HUSBAND to see what he was doing or if he was coming home. He knew we were married. He said it as if he was walking out of the door to go get in my car. I couldn't eat. My stomach was in knots. Cigarettes were my best friend. I was smoking back-to-back. Price called at 6:45 am Monday morning. He meant to come home. He set his alarm clock for 5:30 am, but it didn't go off. The cherry on this pie of deceit was in the mix of his adultery, he got the car impounded. Something about parking in the wrong spot. He didn't have any money and it was MY car. I had to pay $175. What in the world had I done to deserve this? He didn't even acknowledge his wrongdoing. He just kept going like everything was cupcakes and candy. I couldn't have my car sitting at an impound. I agreed to pay for it. It wasn't like I really had a choice anyway.

I was sitting on the couch when he walked through the door. To my surprise, Samar was with him. I stood up. Price said, "Sam this is Samar. Samar, this is Sam." I couldn't believe my eyes. Samar nodded and smiled and sat down on the couch, like it was okay. My jaw was hanging. I was in a state of shock. Price kissed my forehead and thanked me for not going off and being understanding. I couldn't say anything. He brought the boy in our house that, for the last two days, he'd been fucking. He really had the nerve. Then the boy was sickly, skinny and sitting on my couch like that's where he belonged. I lit another cigarette and took a seat in disbelief. Price rolled a blunt to break the tension. I smoked, of course, but I was shaking mad. I knew the entire situation was wrong. I loved my husband, so I went with it. When the blunt was done, I gave him the information he needed to get the car, and they left. It took him two hours to get the car. When he came in, he took a shower and left right back out to go to work.

While he was gone, I called LaShenia and planned my escape. I had to leave. I didn't know what may happen. I was angry as fuck. Price returned home and said he wasn't going to be able to work for that company because he had to do a drug test. I sat Price down in an effort to fix whatever the problem was. I loved my husband, dumb or not. I did. I wanted us to work. I said a few things regarding the job. When I started talking about the last three days, he cut me off. Told me he was a grown ass man and could do what the fuck he wanted. If I wanted to leave, then I could leave because he didn't need me. I already helped him financially, got him out of Minnesota, and he already showed me all the love he could show my stupid ass. I just broke down. I was speechless. He tore my heart right out of my chest. At that point, I didn't care what he chose to do. I knew I wasn't footing the bill for anything anymore. I was leaving.

He continued to throw stones. He called me a prostitute and a sex addict. He said I was lucky he even wanted to be bothered with me when I had such a disgusting past. I was dumbfounded. Did he really just go there? I looked him right in the face and said, "Yeah, I used to be a prostitute, but wasn't your father a prostitute, too? What? You mad, because you are out here fucking for free trying to live like we did? You don't even have a fucking job, no money, not even a high school diploma. How dare you bring up my past. My past has been paying for the life your adultering ass is living. Not to mention everything that you were looking for was right in front of your face, but you are too fucking blind."

He was shocked. His only comeback was, "Fuck you." Then he got up and sat on the balcony.

We didn't speak for the rest of the day. I couldn't even look at him. Price decided he would sleep in the second bedroom. I was just fine with that. But he didn't go to sleep. Samar called and he got dressed to leave. I was dialing LaShenia and my mother-in-law when I heard the keys jingle. I snatched them from him and told him if he wanted to go, he better have Samar come pick him up or he could walk. The phone connected to his mother. She heard all the commotion. I was telling her and LaShenia what was going on, and Price took the phone. He told them that he'd been trying to break up with me for the longest. I was stupid and too damn insecure for him. He threw the phone at me and proceeded to walk out the door. I cried out, "Price I love you dude!" He just kept right on walking and with Tabby on his shoulder. He came back to the house around four o'clock Tuesday morning and went straight to bed. I was over it. I started taking my clothes out of the closet and dresser drawers. Something had to give.

It was April 20th, "National Weed Smoking Day". Despite all the drama, I wanted to go out and get high. Price said there was a barbecue somewhere he was attending with Samar. Go figure. I wasn't about to sit in the house again. I was going crazy. If he was going somewhere and meeting people, I wanted to go. He was my husband. I wanted to go out and meet people with him. He put up a fight at first, but then said I could go. We went to a park instead. It was actually just Price, Samar and I. One of Samar's friends met us there; I paid for the food we were grilling. It was chilly outside and everyone had a jacket except for Price. He was shaking so I tried to make him warm. He dismissed me when I tried to sit on his lap. He said he was tired of doing the same thing with me and I was blowing his high. I was disgusted, he was shewing and blowing me off in front of people; someone he was fucking nonetheless. I tried to hide my pain. If a blunt wasn't lit, I was smoking a cigarette. I didn't eat any of the food. I still wasn't hungry. After everyone ate I invited them back to the apartment. I knew Price would still want to be around them. I figured that was the best way to get him to stay home. Price, Samar and his friend, and I smoked two blunts before Samar's friend was ready to leave. Price walked her out and Samar took the opportunity to talk to me.

"Price told me y'all were having issues, mainly about sex. He wanted a versatile guy, and you weren't masculine enough."

Really? A versatile guy? Like he wanted someone who was bottom and a top? "Did you fuck Price?"

"You would have to ask Price, that sweetheart."

"Well you basically told me already." I was steaming, "You sitting in my fucking house telling me you fucked my husband! That's what the fuck you're doing right now?"

Samar stood up. I was raising my voice. He should have been trying to get out the door.

"Look, you seem like a nice guy. I think you should just leave. Price made you out to be some kind of control freak monster. You don't seem like that at all. He said he is only with you for convenience. He's not *in love* with you. You just make living the lifestyle he wants easy."

I knew he wasn't lying. Price told me the same thing after that entire New Year debacle. He said his love had dwindled away. He cared about me but was not *in love* with me. He honestly didn't know what real love was. He'd never been in love with anyone. I didn't want to believe it then, but now it was coming out of his lover's mouth.

I felt like knocking the shit out of Samar. He was 5'10" maybe 110 pounds soaking wet. I knew I could kill him, but I didn't. I respected him for not coming at me bogus. Price made the decision to cheat, whether Samar knew about me or not, it really wasn't his fault. Plus, he said Price asked him to do a threesome with us. I could see how he would think it was okay to walk into my home and act the way he did. He thought I was going to be cool with it. Price walked in the door. I confronted him while Samar was sitting there. I didn't want him to be able to deny it. He didn't deny it, nor did he acknowledge it. He simply left. Said he was going to Samar's, and he didn't feel like my headache.

******

168

As soon as the leasing office opened, I called to ask how much it would be to break the lease. All My Son's Moving Company was already on their way. I wanted to make sure there were no loose ends. To my surprise Price was already there. The leasing agent told me to come to the office. When I walked in, he was being a true bitch, showing out in the leasing office and really getting on my nerves. I was drained. I didn't have enough strength for his bullshit. I'd been up four days, still had not eaten and my body was going through changes. I just wanted to get away from him. He told the leasing office that the lease did not need to be broken. My name just needed to be removed. I was completely fine with that, no money out of my pocket. We walked out. He got into Samar's truck with two other people and pulled off.

The moving company arrived about nine o'clock in the morning. I was ready. Price was with Samar and two other guys. I didn't know if they would try to jump me, so I informed the two-man crew of the situation and what may transpire. They were understanding and told me to let them know if I saw them coming. They had my back and wouldn't allow anyone to jump me.

I was going to completely empty the house. I took all the furniture and threw all of the food in the dumpster. He didn't need me for anything, so he didn't need my stuff either. We were just about done when Price and Samar pulled up. There were only a few things like the microwave, computer chair and some knick-knacks left in the house, and the way he was acting when he pulled up, I didn't even bother to try and get them.

If the scene in the leasing office wasn't enough, he jumped out the truck cursing and acting a fool. When he came into the apartment and saw everything gone, including the food, he really went ballistic and called me every kind of bitch. He kept screaming that he was ready for me to get the fuck out because I was being so petty. He then told me to give him his fucking house keys. I handed them over with no fight. I was ready to go. He couldn't knock me down any further than he already had. Dealing with Price alone wasn't enough. I apparently deserved worse. When I walked out the door, Samar smiled at me and told me to drive safely. I just gave him a nasty look and got into my car.

SEVENTEEN

ESCAPE FROM HELL

Destination: San Diego, California! I needed SUNSHINE! I was in a terrible way and ready for something new. The furniture was going to storage. I certainly wasn't going to take it to California. We unloaded the furniture into the storage unit. I did some last minute running around. I had to go to the cable company and drop off the boxes and ensure they knew I did not live at that address any longer. I went to Best Buy to get a GPS and more music since Price threw all of my CDs out of the window. I routed my trip to California. It was six o'clock in the evening on April 21. I hadn't slept in five days. I was about to embark on a twenty-two hour trip. Newport's and Red Bull would help me get down the road.

With tear filled eyes, I popped in my new Mary J. Blige CD, *Stronger* and started my journey. I drove ten hours and cried the entire time. I stopped when I reached the border of Texas and New Mexico because LaShenia insisted I get a hotel room. It was a waste of money more than anything. I got there around four o'clock Thursday morning. I couldn't sleep and being still in the hotel room alone was not good for me. My mind was playing tricks on me. My imagination was haunting me. Vivid images of Price with Samar kept appearing in front of my eyes. I could hear them laughing at me. I felt like the butt of a big joke. He hadn't even called while I was driving. He was with another man and was not thinking about me. My mind was running. I couldn't stop thinking. No matter how hard I tried or how tight I closed my eyes, the tears kept coming and the thoughts ran rapid.

Soon enough it turned to self-hatred. It couldn't have been Price's fault I wasn't worth loving. He loved me in the beginning. Apparently I was not doing enough to satisfy him. *How could I expect someone to stay with me I couldn't truly provide for and make happy? He deserved better. I wasn't masculine. I didn't listen to rap. I listened to "bitch" music. Was I tripping? This couldn't be my fault. I loved Price with my entire being. I loved my husband. I tried so hard to make it work. Maybe I didn't try hard enough. I did just leave him in Dallas with strangers. Something could happen to him. What if he gets hurt? I could never live with myself.*

I kept shaking my head and contradicting myself. *Get it together Sam.* Something could just as easily happen to you. It was true. I was the one suffering from sleep deprivation and damn near starvation. How would I be able to trust anyone ever again? I was left without a husband, friend and lover. I knew that I couldn't deal with heartbreak like this again. Men were dogs. I loved Price and hated him at the same time. The entire situation had me stuck in a twilight zone. I even considered going straight. The realist side of me knew that that wasn't cool. I didn't really want to be with a woman, and I'll be damned if I was going to become a DL nigga. What if someone did the same thing to my nieces or younger cousins? I learned from my relationship with Adonis not to play with anyone's heart. Cigarette after cigarette and Red Bulls back-to-back, I wanted sleep but my head hurt. I had to keep moving! If I stayed still, I cried. If I moved, I cried. If I laughed, took a piss, wiped my nose, or even pumped gas, I cried. I was sitting in the hotel room for three hours crying. There was no point in losing any more time. I wasn't going to sleep. At seven o'clock, I got back on the road.

******

The last 12 hours down the road weren't so bad. LaShenia comforted me through prayer and uplifting conversation. She let me know she was there for me and would help rebuild my life. I was so broken. I didn't know how to feel about anything. My heart was numb and my mind was a circus. I'd been awake for seven days and still no food, I looked sick, and I could tell I was smaller. The realization that I was literally killing myself over someone who didn't give a fuck about me made me cry even harder. I couldn't get myself together. I was experiencing the worst stomach pains. My eyes were burning. I was pissing acid and couldn't go to the bathroom. The thought of chewing and swallowing took too much energy from my lifeless body. I could not fathom actually doing it.

It's a miracle I made it to my sister's door. I went straight to the door. I didn't even grab my bags. I just wanted to feel the warmth of someone who loved me. She answered the door with open arms and held me for over five minutes. I was crying like a big baby, and LaShenia was my mother. She held me and rocked me. She rubbed my head and assured me everything was going to be okay. Then my 12-year-old niece came and held me from the side and started crying too. It hurt me to see my family hurt, but it warmed my heart to know that someone truly did care and was right there waiting for me. After I gathered myself, and everyone else got it together, we brought the bags in the house. LaShenia and I spoke briefly about my plan. She promised she would help me spiritually, mentally, emotionally and financially, but decisions and choices would be my own. I felt a sense of relief in her presence. It was like she was going to protect me and everything was going to be okay. Surprisingly, I yawned, and finally, I fell asleep.

I awoke to the smell of bacon, eggs, and pancakes. I could even smell the syrup and grits. My stomach was ready. LaShenia kept my nieces home from school that Friday. She said they were going to surround me with love. Missing one day wouldn't hurt. Love is exactly what I got. When I walked into the kitchen, my nieces were there, my brother-in-law and, of course, LaShenia. They welcomed me with opened arms and good food. Boy was I hungry. We spent the rest of the day getting me and my things settled in and talking about life. Saturday was peaceful and relaxing. Sunday we went to church. The entire house went to church. Going to church after so many years was heavy enough as it was, when I accepted why I'd really come, I broke all the way down. I was hurt. I had been beaten, battered, torn and discarded. I was embarrassed. I felt worthless. I felt like a quitter. I should have stayed with my husband regardless of what he had done or said. I loved him. I married him. I wanted to stand by my vows, but he didn't want to stand by his. I fell to my knees and cried hard and loud. I didn't care who saw. I wanted the Lord to take away the pain. I needed him to understand just how deep it was. My other half was gone. I was left with half of my soul. I loved him with all my heart. I couldn't believe my marriage was over in just a year and nine months. We couldn't even make it to our two-year anniversary. I "pled" to the Lord to free me from my anguish. I would take heed to his warnings and live right if he would just free me from my anguish.

******

I was in California for a week when I made the decision to cut my hair. I was 31 years old, and I had it long for the majority of my life. I was starting fresh and new. A new look was only right. I didn't want to seem feminine anymore. I was gay and had no problem admitting it. There was no need for long swinging hair and long fingernails.

I tried to call my voicemail and found my password had been changed. I went to the Sprint store and was informed I was ordering new phones on a new line. That's why I couldn't access my voicemail. Once I explained that that was indeed false, I checked my voicemail and found out Price somehow managed to reopen the credit card we shared under my company name. Price was a sneaky bastard. I closed all the joint accounts and credit cards he had access to while I was driving to California, yet and still, he found away to get to my money. He even raised the limit. I also learned he opened his electricity account in my name. He cashed a $700 check made out to me. He had forged my signature and signed it over to himself. I was in complete disbelief. Price was trying to steal my identity.

By mid-May, he spent the entire check and almost $5,000 on the credit card. I got a phone call from a friend at the credit union that I used to work at in Minnesota informing me a man called and tried to have my account closed. The man said he was Samuel P. Holloway, III and requested a check for $10,000 be sent to his address in Dallas. Little did the person calling know, the operator on the phone knew me. I also had put a password on the account when I left Dallas. I changed my address to my sister's address in California. The man was unable to verify the password or new

175

address and hung up on her. That's when she called me. I was mad but tickled at the same time. Price had just finished telling me he didn't need me for anything. Here he was trying to take everything that belonged to me. Silly rabbit didn't he know tricks were for kids? I filed a complaint for identity theft and asked her to send me a certified, notarized letter stating exactly what happened. Bank calls were usually recorded. If it came down to it, I could find a way to get the recording if the letter wasn't enough.

******

I wanted the world to know what Price did to me, but my 300+ friends on *Facebook* would have to suffice. I was posting everything on my page. All of it was true, no slander or defamation, just the cold hard facts.

Luciano saw the postings and sent me a *Facebook* message: "Sam what are all these postings about? You guys have gotten into it before and have broken up. It always worked out. Y'all are married, and he knows the grass is not greener on the other side of town. I met you before. I know you're a cool person. Work that shit on out."

My first few encounters with Luciano weren't pleasant. His telephone number was one of two I found the first time I went through Price's wallet. When I called it, I found out he was Price's ex-boyfriend. At one point, I actually drove to Chicago to fight him. Since we've settled our differences, I was happy he hit me up. He knew Price the way I did, that's the kind of person I needed to talk to. I responded to his message with my phone number.

He called right away, and I was happy. We talked every day for three days before I noticed the change in his voice. I was so consumed with my own problems; I didn't even ask Luciano what was going on with him.

"Luciano, what's up with you? Where you at?"

He hesitated.

"Luciano, what's wrong dude? I've just been pouring my heart to you. You know you can talk to me."

"I'm in West Virginia. I have AIDS Sam. I've had ***PCP phenomena*** for a while, they think I'm dying."

I felt bad. "Is anyone there with you?"

"No."

He was in the hospital and thought he was going to die but had no family by his side. I felt a connection with him. I knew he'd been with Price before and after we broke up the first time. That could very well be either one of us in the hospital. I was breaking down. I asked him if I could tell my sister. He said sure. LaShenia and I began to pray for Luciano. We cried together. I told him I was going to come out there. I felt like he didn't need to be alone. I was his friend. I was here for him.

LaShenia found a flight while we were on the phone. I told Luciano to get some sleep, and I let him know I would be there in the morning.

******

LaShenia took me to the airport. I called Price before I boarded my flight. I just wanted to tell him what was going on with Luciano. He told me he was busy in bed. Samar I assumed. I was fighting back tears and asked that he please call Luciano. He was sick. He could at least show him some support. He started cursing. He called me stupid for going to see Luciano because he didn't really like me. He just had no one else. He went on to say he would call when and if he felt like it.

I arrived in West Virginia and took a taxicab to the hospital. I walked to the nurse's desk and told them I was there to see my brother Luciano in 305. I gathered myself for whatever I was going to see behind the door and walked into the room. Luciano looked horrible. He was plugged into several different tubes and on a breathing machine. He was very little. It looked like he weighed under 100 pounds. He cracked a weak smile. I bent over the bed to hug him. We both started crying. He was heavily medicated and very weak. It made him comfortable knowing someone who loved him was by his side. I sat down. I told him I wasn't much of a church go'er nor did I read the *Bible* every day, but my sister gave me some scriptures to read to him. He smiled at the thought. Said he would love for me to read them. I read a few scriptures and before long he was sleeping.

I felt so horrible inside. Luciano was dying and the only person who cared enough to be there was his "ex-boyfriend's husband" whom at one point, he was going to fight. I couldn't imagine it. I broke down. What if I was lying there, and Price said fuck me and did not come to my side? If he left me sick and weak? If he went on with his life and wasn't thinking about me except for if he was in need? I called my backbone, LaShenia. I needed someone to keep me strong, so I could continue to be strong for Luciano. LaShenia and I prayed for Luciano while I rubbed his head and wiped the sweat away from his body. He was coughing and I could hear when he'd stop breathing and gasp for air. I knew I had to find away to lift his spirits. He was now like my little brother. I was going to be here by his side until whatever happened. Nurses were coming in and out of the room checking his vitals and putting medicine in his IV's. I fell asleep. When I opened my eyes the next morning, a doctor was in the room going over his vitals. I took the opportunity to ask him questions about Luciano's condition. He explained the hard details but closed the conversation by letting me know that Luciano had improved overnight. He was breathing better. His temperature was going down, but he was still in the red zone. I was happy there was improvement.

We talked about everything from GOD and the *Bible* to life and death. We compared our lives. We talked about Price. I found out so many things I didn't know. Price told me he moved to Minnesota because he got a job. As it turned out, according to Luciano he moved because Luciano was cheating on him and he didn't want to be around him anymore. He also told me that he was a top. That meant when Price was with him he was the girl. That explained the bitch fits and voguing. He apologized for being an intruder in my relationship. He said he knew it was wrong. He had so much respect for me because he'd done things with Price while he was my boyfriend and husband, but I still came to be with him in his time of need. That's when I found out he and Price had Webcam sex while we were together, and that he sent Price money from time to time. He apologized for being mischievous and helping Price hurt me. I couldn't be mad at him. It was not all his fault. His loyalty was to himself and Price. Price's loyalty was supposed to be to me.

We made amends of all our indiscretions towards each other. I didn't care about what once was. I just wanted Luciano to get better and if he wasn't going to, I didn't want him to think I was mad with him about anything. I kept praying for him. Every time he went to sleep I prayed over him. I didn't know exactly what some of the scriptures meant, but I felt the presence of GOD in the room. I kept a strong faith in my friend's recovery. Luciano complained of muscle pains so I massaged his body while we talked and as he slept. The night passed and a chipper and excited voice woke me up. "Sam wake up, I'm hungry." I'll never forget those words and the smile on Luciano's face. We busted out laughing. Then he looked at me and said, "Man, I feel so good!" That made me feel amazing and when the doctor came in the day got even brighter.

He said it was a miracle. Most people that are in the condition Luciano was in don't walk out. Luciano told the doctor he'd do one better. He'd run out. We all laughed. The doctor told him he was a very lucky young man and he'd just dodged a bullet. His lungs still have some spots, but they were clearing up. He no longer needed the breathing machine. His temperature was steady at 99 degrees, and he had gained three pounds. But he was still in the red zone. We thanked GOD and prayed some more. Luciano was feeling much better. He got dressed, and we went to eat at the McDonald's down stairs. In the elevator he made a comment about how he could walk and felt good. Just some days earlier, he couldn't even walk to the bathroom without getting tired, and it was only a few steps away from the bed. I was just as excited; he looked seven times better than he did when I got there.

I was set to leave the following day. His spirit seemed so lifted. I didn't think it was a good time to depart. I changed my flight to leave a couple of days later. We made great memories, laughed and prayed. I watched him get better. As much as I wanted to be there when he left, I had to go handle my own life. I didn't leave without a testimony. I knew GOD was good. He saved my friend Luciano. He walked in that hospital knocking on death's door and walked out thanking GOD to be alive.

******

I was back in California for a couple of days when Price called. At first he seemed friendly. He wanted something I could tell. So I got to the point and asked, what's up? He immediately got defensive and called me stupid again for going to see Luciano. He said I thought I was cute and big shit because I was traveling but he fucked me more than I even knew and he fucking hated me. What else was new? He was more confused than I was. Why call if he hated me so much?

By July, I had driven to Dallas four times to see Price. The trip in July made five. When I got there, I gave him $300 because he didn't have his half of the rent. His best friend Tony moved to Dallas and took the second bedroom in the apartment I left. I guess he thought that would make it easier to pay bills. But he was still evicted and ended up moving into Terry's apartment. LaShenia didn't like that I was helping Price or going to see him, but he was my husband. I felt I had to make an effort to keep us together. When we talked, he wasn't mean. We were on a better note.

He told me he missed me. He wanted me home. I wanted to be home. BJ was a straight boy I considered a best friend. He was there for me during times of need. When I was lonely, his family welcomed me. He wanted to move to Dallas to go to barber school and open a business. I figured that was a perfect reason to move back to Dallas. Plus, I got offered a position at North Dallas Bank. I moved back. I knew things were going to be right this time, and I was ready to reconcile my marriage. LaShenia warned me against it but left the ultimate decision up to me. After three months in San Diego, in August, I moved back to Dallas.

When I got there, BJ was trying to settle in. It wasn't long before he found out he wasn't eligible for financial aid and wasn't going to start school. That put a damper on things. He was my excuse for coming back to Dallas and without him there I was left alone with Price again. It was what it was. BJ went back to Minnesota. Things were simple and smooth the first couple of weeks. Price introduced me to some other people he met. There were three women and six guys. They seemed cool. One stood out the most. He was tall, 6'2" or 6'3", 210 pounds, toffee brown complexion and dark brown eyes. He wasn't my type. But his big friendly smile and hospitable demeanor drew me to him. He was from Arkansas. I would definitely call him country. He was cute and sweet, his name was Damion, and with him and everyone else we created a little friendship circle. I was settling right in.

I went on the interview and declined the job. They didn't want to give me a management position. I felt I had too much experience for less. I had been in banking for eleven years. I was in management for four of the eleven years, an assistant manager for three and a branch manager for one. I was not going to be a teller. I didn't need the money. I still had the rental property and money from my 401K, so I was good. Price, on the other hand, was not so good and moved in with me. I still did not trust him. He was sleeping on my couch, not in my bed. I wanted to be with him, but before I got too comfortable, I had to do my research. He had been in Dallas for three months alone. I had no clue what kind of stuff he may have gotten into. One night while he was asleep on the couch I went through his phone. There were no sent messages only received. I read all of them and to my surprise, Tony, Price's best friend, was a major player in the fun Price was having in Dallas. I knew that was "Karma." I did the same thing to April, Adonis' girlfriend. I didn't know her like Tony knew me, but I was sleeping with her boyfriend and smiling in her face every time she came to the credit union.

I went in the living room and woke him up. "You need to get ya shit and get the fuck out my house!"

He jumped up with a confused look. He was just sleeping. "What time is it dude? What the hell are you talking about? I'm trying to sleep."

I knew he was trying to sleep but I woke his ass up and for a good reason, he needed to leave.

"Price, you have been fucking everyone in Dallas," I threw the phone at him, "You have somewhere else to go—asked Tony or ask Brandon. I don't care who you've ask. You just need to leave."

"What the hell are you mad for? We are not together."

That reality hurt, but he had a point. Still, I had moved back to Dallas to be with him. The entire time I was in California being nice and trying to put fourth effort to fix our marriage, he was getting down with everyone he introduced me to, except for Damion.

I reiterated that I wanted him gone. He told me to go fuck myself and started walking towards the bedroom. I was not about to let him go back to sleep, not in my apartment. I followed him. I was sick of him ignoring me. I was fed up with him not acknowledging my presence and my concerns. I was getting angrier by the minute. He was packing his stuff. I was in his face mentioning all the things I'd done to make us work. Everything he was doing was pulling us apart. I think the problem with Price was he didn't really know just how crazy I was in high school. He put his hands on me and in my face no less. I smacked the shit out of Price. I grabbed his keys in an effort to take my apartment key and car key off his chain. He came behind me, picked me up and slammed me to the ground on my head. I laid there dazed, confused and crying. He was walking away but realized he actually hurt me and came back. He was standing over me and tried to pick me up. I didn't know what he was going to do. I grabbed him in defense mode. Once we were up, he threw me into the brick wall, and I flipped him around and threw him into the wall.

He ran and grabbed his phone, screaming now I was going to see what it felt like to sit in jail. He was calling the police and told them I had attacked him because he didn't want to be with me. He was trying to pack his things to leave. "What a bitch." I wasn't going to jail. I grabbed my phone and called the police too. I told them he was on the other line lying to the police, trying to have me arrested. I was putting him out. He didn't want to leave and was trying to take possessions that weren't his. He hit me, and he was locked up before in Minnesota for domestic battery a year ago.

DPD (Dallas Police Department) didn't play. They were there within minutes. There were four officers. Two of them took Price outside. The other two came inside with me. They questioned us both. I showed them the gash that was on my back shoulder from when he pushed me into the wall. Both of us had blood on our shirts, and they were torn and stretched. The police questioned my story because Price had marks around his neck from me choking him and a smack mark on his face. I told them he hit me first. I told them exactly how it played out. He muffled me, so I smacked him. They decided to take him to jail because he hit me first.

They put Price in handcuffs, and he looked at me with puppy dog eyes and asked if I was really going to send him to jail again. I told him he shouldn't have put his hands on me. That night he called crying and told me how sorry he was. I knew we were not going to be together. I didn't want him sitting in jail. I still loved him. So I paid the $1,500 and bailed him out of jail. He came back to my house but was only there a week before he walked away. It was time. There was no life left in our relationship. He didn't want to leave Tabby with me. He didn't have a place of his own, and everyone wasn't receptive to cats. I told him Tabby was my cat just like he was his. We've had him for two years now. He was like my child for real. I had no problem keeping him because I didn't want him to end up homeless like Price. He emphasized that we were done and asked that I leave him and his mother alone. I could work on not speaking to him. He knew I loved his mom like she was my own, she'd accepted me like I was her own and with the strenuous relationship I had, had with my own mother, she was the motherly figure I needed in my life. I know I said I was okay with Price's leaving, but I honestly wasn't. I pleaded with him not to leave. I felt like we could work things out. He was all I knew for the last three and a half years. I really didn't know how I could live without him. I pleaded profusely. He still walked away.

When he was walking out the door, he turned around like Celie from *The Color Purple*.

"You're gonna fail, watch. All of my ex's fail after fucking with me. I am the best thing that ever happened to any of y'all. Who cares if I want to sit on my ass? I look fine as hell. Anyone would want to take care of me!"

I told him all I wanted was all of him. I gave him my soul, and I wanted his in return. I didn't feel like that was a lot to ask from my husband.

"It was just sex. That's all, Samuel, just sex. But don't worry," he said as he walked out the door and got into the new dudes car, "You're gonna get everything that you deserve soon enough."

Price was really gone, but I lived in Dallas and needed to embrace it so I started hanging out with the boys I met again. I couldn't depend on Price. I couldn't sit in the house and be a do-nothing. I started going out. Around mid-October, I was invited to a house party with this boy Thomas.

He knew the guy that was throwing it, and it was going to be live, and said I should go with him. The party was in Oak Cliff, a suburb of Dallas, where there were lots of other gay men. We got high on the way there. When we walked in I was zoned. There were a lot of cute boys and not so cute boys. One boy in particular was really eyeing me. It was a strange stare though. He didn't look like he was interested in me. He looked like he had a problem with me. I asked Thomas if he noticed. He asked me if knew him. I didn't. So I walked over to the boy,

"Excuse me. I don't know if you have me confused with someone, but you look like you have a problem or something. I just moved here from California and didn't have any issues with anyone."

The boy looked at me and smirked, "California, really? Naw, you just moved here from Minnesota." My heart dropped, as I really didn't know anyone in Dallas. This boy knew I was in Minnesota. I was trying to recall his face, but I couldn't.

"I know you, I used to fuck with Price. You fucked him over, and because of you he doesn't want a relationship with someone real. Someone like me—someone who will cut for they nigga."

I didn't know what he was talking about. I knew who Price was, but I didn't know who fucked him over. I didn't. "No, none of that is true! That's just Price. It has nothing to do with you. You don't know me, so we don't even have to speak about it."

"You took all that boy's shit. Took his car, his furniture, got him fired from his job and cleaned out his bank account and to top it off, you used to be a whore, and you cheated on him".

Seemed like the music stopped. All the men in the room were looking at us. I was uncomfortable. I didn't know this boy, nor did

I know anyone else there except Thomas and I really didn't know him. I wasn't trying to get jumped in Dallas I just told him what Price told him was what he did to me. He only knew one side. He shouldn't have an issue with me because he did not know me or the situation. Then I told Thomas I was ready to go because I was very paranoid.

******

Four other strangers in Dallas approached me with the Price story. They all saw my picture and knew who I was because Price was showing it to everyone and telling his story: I stole everything and left him stranded. Apparently that's how he was surviving, by dogging my name. Price and I were still speaking. He moved right around the corner from me. I told him about the party and people I met. He claimed he didn't know who the people I met were. He had no clue whatsoever who the boy was from the party. He told people his story because they asked. He told nothing but the truth. I disagreed. He threw me under the bus to strangers. He lied on me. He showed people my face and told them about my very distinctive black and white Mitsubishi. The main point was that the story he was telling was not his life. Chicago, Minnesota, being jobless; not having a pot to piss in or a window to throw it out of; that was his story but not with him on the higher end of the relationship. He left me and described a monster to everyone. I couldn't be bothered with him.

I tried not to think about the nonsense. Damion and I were speaking on a regular basis. I told him I needed to find a church because when I am part of a church I feel much better. The last Sunday in October we went to the Inspiring Body of Christ, Church (IBOC) together. Pastor Rush delivered a sermon titled

"The Enemy Was About to Attack." He stated that some of us were in "the valley" and didn't know it. It was going to take a drastic situation to make us see that we really have to let go of negative people around us.

Move away from situations that are blocking our blessings. Some of us turn away from a situation and turn back when we know we shouldn't because they would block your blessings. Some of us were not in the right place to be blessed. Some of us left the place of blessings and have not received any since.

This was exactly what I needed. I knew he was talking directly to me. Before I left Minnesota I was being blessed. Once we arrived in Dallas, all my blessings immediately stopped. When I went to California with my sister, all my blessings returned right away. I moved back to Dallas and since I've been here, no blessings. I just had a load of confusion. It was very spiritual and healing. It allowed me to see the inner side of me. I realized what needed to be done, so I could "harvest my seed."

While I was in California, I posted a simple story about myself on Facebook. I had been trying to write my book for years, but I never had the "sit down time" to get into it. My cousin's friend Mina was a publisher and contacted me to see if I was serious about writing my book. She told me she would publish it if I was serious and I should think of coming to Atlanta. It sounded like a good deal, but I had other things on my mind. I could have easily stayed in California. I could have even gone back to Minnesota with the other half of my family. But I loved Price. I wanted to be with him regardless of what I was going through with him. He was my everything, but chasing him seemed opposite of the preacher's sermon. My book was my "seed." I needed to harvest it. I was offered a deal and walked away from it, so I could be with a man who didn't want to be with me. I was in a dark place. It was my fault. I wasn't acknowledging my blessing. I needed to. I was on a cloud after church. I knew what it was I needed to do , and I was ready to be on the move. I was going to reconnect with Mina and start writing my book because I had to get the information out there.

CHAPTER EIGHTEEN

A LONG WAY DOWN

On November 2, 2010, I went to the gas station down the street from my apartment off the North Beltline Toll way to get some gas and blunt wraps. I saw a boy with a familiar face. He recognized me from the house party Thomas and I attended. He was about 5'9" and brown skinned, wore clean sneakers and a chill fit. He was hard too. He wasn't my type, but he seemed cool and laid back. He introduced himself as Charles and asked if I smoked. Of course I did. He said we should chill. I didn't see anything wrong with that, so we exchanged numbers. He said after he got some weed he would hit me up. We could meet back at the gas station then I could follow him to his house. That sounded good to me. I went home, rolled up and waited for him to call.

About an hour later, Charles called and said he was ready to match a blunt. I left out and headed to the gas station. When I pulled in, he was standing at a gas pump without a car. I didn't think anything of it. Since I needed gas, I pulled up to the pump, and he got in. We were chatting in the car when I noticed a car pull up behind me. There were six gas pumps. I was at the one in the back. The one in front of me was available, but if they wanted to sit behind me that was fine. I got out to get gas. I was looking down digging in my pocket to get my wallet when I felt the gun at the back of my head. My heart started racing. This was the second time I had a gun to my head. This situation was definitely different. He told me not to turn around. He wanted the cash, jewelry and my wallet. I told him I didn't carry cash. I tried to turn around.

I woke up in the back seat of my car lying on my back. I could see trees out the back window. I was no longer at the gas station. My head was pounding. The front seats were pushed up as far as they could go. Charles was no longer in the car, and a boy was sitting on my abdomen. I was trying to focus in but my head was throbbing and my vision was blurred. He unscrewed my one-karat diamond earrings and told me I was about to die. Told me he was going to make sure I never have the chance to fuck over anyone else. I saw the back of the gun sitting in the window above me. My first thought was to reach for it, but my left arm was pinned under his legs. I didn't know if my right hand could reach because it was between my body and the seat back. Oh Lord, I could see clearly. I realized who it was. It was the guy from the party in Oak Cliff. The look on his face was pure evil. I'll never forget it. I couldn't help but think I was going to die.

I started crying and begging for my life, "*You don't have to kill me. I don't have any family in Dallas. You don't have to kill me. I'll give you anything you want and leave the state. I won't even say anything about this. Please, you don't have to kill me!*"

He didn't care about anything I was saying, "All I want is Price, I can't have him because of you Bitch! Shut the fuck up cause you are about to die. You want to talk? Start saying your prayers."

Say my prayers? My prayers? Oh my GOD!? How did I get into this? Price? All this for Price? I thought I would die for him. When it came down to it, I wanted to live. I WANTED TO LIVE! I knew this boy was serious. If I wasn't going to make it, I was going to fight for my life. I wanted some kind of DNA on me, so I hit him as hard as I could with my right hand, broke my finger and sprained my wrist. He hit me in my face with the butt of the gun, busting blood vessels in my eyes. I was choking and gasping for air. He turned the gun and placed it to my forehead. I couldn't stop crying. There were so many things running through my head. Was this how I was going to end? Was this my story? He was going to blow my head off in the back seat of my car, because he was in love with my husband.

He was talking, but I couldn't hear him. My mind was searching for peace. The only thoughts that came into my head were about my nieces, nephew, and Tabby. I knew the next time they saw me would be in a casket. I closed my eyes.

P O P...

He pulled the trigger. I was still here ... Images of Romie and LaShenia in my head. I cried out and started praying aloud Romans 8:28: and we know that all things work together for good to them that love GOD..."

POP...

to them who are called according to his purpose. He shot me again in the middle of my prayer. I was still here. My family and friends popped into my head. I felt bad. My family loved me and told me not to move to Dallas. They told me to let the situation die. Here I was about to do just that. I continued to cry and ask him not to kill me. He had shot the gun twice already. I wasn't gone. I didn't want to be.

Then I heard the guy outside the car with a hat on. Tell him to hurry the fuck up and quit playing. The boy told him he was trying, but the gun kept jamming. He was evil, pure rage. I saw the devil's face that night. He was so mad I wouldn't die. My heart couldn't take anymore.

POP... POP

"He will never forsake you...Trust, believe and always have faith in HIM," and he shall set you free. GOD was watching over me and Keisha must have been blocking the bullets because I was still here. He did not like that at all. He started beating me with the gun in my face. All along the right side of my body. He wanted me dead. He wanted me to feel pain, all I could do was lie there. I was in the devil's dungeon. He was having his way with me. Price. Price. Price. He was ranting about Price. He told Price he would ***cut*** for him. I was going to die, one way or another! The pain was unimaginable. He beat me hard and mercilessly. I could see the blood spatter and feel the burns every time my skin was sliced open. It was excruciating.

Cut—Dallas slang meaning I'll kill someone for you

******

"Are you alive? Have you been shot? Young man have you been shot? Bill, he's alive. We have to drive him to the hospital?"

I thought it was an angel's voice. I couldn't see a face. My right eye wouldn't open. My left eye was blurry. I felt wet, like a bucket of water was thrown on me. There was so much blood on me. I could barely move my arm. My body was throbbing from head to toe. I could tell the car was moving. Thank GOD they left the keys. The driver told me that everything was going to be okay and hang in there. We were on the way to the hospital. We got to the hospital, and I was placed on a gurney. I saw the face of my personal angels, an older white couple. I thanked GOD for them and for my life.

I woke up in a hospital bed alone. It was ironic. I sat by Luciano's side when he thought he was going to die, and here I was, almost dead and alone. I thought about many different circumstances because part of me did die. You can say I was shot four times at point blank range. That boy killed me four times because of a story my husband told him. He killed me because I loved my husband. He killed me. He killed me and walked away and no one even knew I was dead. Reality is I didn't get shot. My guardian angel and GOD did not allow me to die. As much as I didn't want to place this particular call, I was in Dallas. He was my only family there. I called Price and told him what happened. If I were supposed to be learning a lesson, I definitely was. Price's reaction was so nonchalant I couldn't help but cry. He didn't come to the hospital. I was there four days. He didn't even call back to check on me.

I was released on November 6, I had no cell phone, no wallet, no jewelry and most of all no pride. I had just been beaten up and almost killed by a guy who had, had sex with my husband. My husband wasn't even by my side. Furthermore, he knew where I lived. I filed a police report. I lived in a gated community, but I was in his territory. ALONE! Three broken ribs, a black eye, rattling teeth, a sprained wrist and a hand broken in two places, cuts and bruises all over the right side of my body, and I could barely walk. I put myself in a cab and went home.

I dragged myself up the steps and knocked on my neighbor's door. When she saw me I cried. The look on her face hurt my heart because I knew I looked horrible. I asked if I could use the phone to call my family and Price. Romie and LaShenia wanted to get on the next flight, but I told them not to come. I didn't want them or any of my family to see me like that. I was embarrassed and ashamed. They were mad and steaming. I didn't want anything to go down on account of me. I told everyone to stay where they were. I couldn't drive and had to be at the dentist at two o'clock that afternoon. I asked Price if he would take me. Finally, he agreed to help. His friend took us to the hospital to get my car. Then he and I drove to the dentist's office. I had to get a wire in my gums to hold my teeth together. They were all loose. I was in so much pain. My body, my mouth and my soul hurt. I didn't know how I was supposed to continue. I did know I was given a second chance. I was not going to waste it chasing false dreams and tainted promises.

On the way home from the dentist, I asked Price if he would come stay with me. The dude who attacked me had my wallet and address. I was honestly scared. "No, I'm with someone else."

I was damn near murdered and beaten in his name and still no emotion. I even said he could bring the person he was with because I had two bedrooms. I just really didn't want to be alone. I was scared for my life. I told him he knew the guy, and I described him in detail. I felt like if he was there and the guy did come over, Price would've been able to stop him from killing me for real. I once heard the saying, "pick a story and stick with it." Well, that's what Price was doing. He claimed no knowledge of this person's existence. He didn't know who I was talking about. I didn't have the energy to argue with Price, no energy at all. I told him either he didn't want to tell me or he didn't remember who he had fucked, because he fucked too many people to remember, or his ass had me set up.

"Don't try and pull a guilt trip on me. You left me here in Dallas alone remember."

He was astounding, he was going to try and make this about him. With tears in my eyes and pain throughout my body, I told him that was different. He was still in good health. He could've gotten a job, and made it. I paid half of his rent, and Tony was there too. Plus he stole all that money from me. He took the credit card and got a $3,000 cash advance. I was still taking care of him even when I was in California coming to visit him. I made sure he was okay, and he couldn't stay with me when a faggot who was "cutting" in his name had just tried to kill me. Fuck it. I thought maybe this was exactly what I was supposed to see. Once he left, I knew I was never going to look at him the same. I did get shot four times in the back of the Gallant. The bullets went into the part of my soul that yearned, craved and loved him. Price was dead to me when he walked out the door. The love was not there anymore.

I laid on that couch, and cried. The pain was unbearable. All I had was Tabby, who no matter what would not leave my side. He just sat there next to me and watched me. He didn't eat. He never left me. When I went to the bathroom, he went to the bathroom. If I cried, he cried. By ten o'clock that night, I knew I had to call someone. I managed to get back to my neighbor's house and called Damion, Brandon and Tion. I told them what happened and to my surprise, all of them came over.

For the next month, I slowly became indebted to them. They sat with me, bathed me, fed me and rotated shifts until I was able to fully walk and drive again. Damion, in particular, was an amazing part of my recovery. If no one else could make it over, he could. I was married and in the same state as my husband but in my time of need, strangers were caring for me. Being completely broken down gave me time to think. I knew it was time for things to change. I was ready to start changing. The first Sunday I was able to go back to church I was there. Damion and I went back to IBOC. Ironically, the pastor's sermon was titled, "The Enemy Has Attacked." I went to the floor and "thank" GOD for his blessings. I was almost killed. I remembered the first time I had attended. He said the enemy was going to attack. It happened. Now this sermon was all about the rainbow after the storm. I joined church immediately. I knew this was my calling. I'd just fallen so far from where I was, or thought I was. It was going to take a lot of rebuilding, focus and determination to get back on my feet completely. GOD gave me a second chance and, like I said, there was no way I was going to mess this up.

Because GOD is an awesome GOD, Mina, the publisher, called me again. She had no idea what happened. So I told her. She said that means it's time for you to come to Atlanta and get that book out. She offered to help me anyway she could. I knew this was my calling. It's meant for me to tell my story to the world and help someone else. Fourteen years ago, I sat with my best friend in front of a prophetess who told me I would be a motivational speaker. I was so young, and not being able to see beyond the reach of my own arm, I didn't believe her. But after years of struggle and life changing events, I knew this is exactly what she was referring to. I knew GOD had not forsaken me.

Considering another move made me think about Price. I was still in love with him regardless of what had transpired. I knew it could never be and would never be again. I will forever cherish our good times. I forgave him for the hurt, pain and suffering he inflicted upon me. Nevertheless, he didn't deserve me. I wasn't going to squander my second chance continuing to chase a boy. I will always love him but from a FAR distance. I was there for him and his family. I had his best interest at heart and put myself on the back burner. I wanted to make him happy in anyway I could. He was all I had and everything I ever wanted. He was that deal. Unfortunately, at his age, he was more concerned with what he had for the moment instead of what he could've had for a lifetime. It left me to wonder. Was what I settled with, worth what I settled for?

Relationships are tricky and scary. People get so wrapped up in their other half that they forget who they are. Price definitely consumed me. I was so wrapped up into him that I forgot about myself. He didn't do anything to me that I didn't allow him too. I had a choice, and I chose to roll with him. I could have walked away the first time he cheated, let alone the second or third time. I could've left when he later divulged that he tested positive for HIV and syphilis. I didn't have to come back from California when I learned he was cheating while I was gone and got syphilis again. Like a fool I stayed because se I loved him unconditionally. But 31 years of struggle and triumphant was not going to end at his hand or the hand of anyone on his behalf.

Dallas was not the place for me. My father's family lived in and around Georgia and soon so would I. It was time for me to live my life for me. That's exactly what I was going to do.

CHAPTER NINETEEN

SUNSHINE

December 31, 2010, I moved into my new home. Mina found it for me and set everything up with the leasing office for my arrival. Damion rode with me from Dallas. My home-boy Steven, from Gary, met us at the apartment. Steven lived in Conyers, Georgia and offered to help me unload and unpack my things. Damion did a turn-around. He got a flight and went right back to Texas. Some things I just couldn't lift, but GOD works in mysterious ways. While Steven and I were unloading the truck, a dude walked by. I asked him for help. His name was Tony or Tee. He was real dark brown, 6'1 or 6'2, an uncommonly deep voice and a back home country accent. He helped move the couch, bed, dining set and TVs with Steven. He was cool. So I asked him if he wanted to hang around and smoke.

******

I was so excited, a brand new year, in a new state with a new attitude. New Year's resolutions were never my style, but I was making some now:

1. Love Samuel like nothing else in the world mattered! I wanted to fall head over heels in love with me. Sweep me off my feet. Take me on nice dates, and buy me fancy things.

2. Write my book. I had a message to deliver and it was my responsibility to do so. I have to get my story out so people can learn from it. Young and old, homosexual and heterosexual, male and female; there's a lesson for everyone in this book. Lives would be affected in a positive way. That's all I could hope for.

3. Don't worry, and be happy. I spent a lot of time sad, crying and miserable. GOD showed me life was too short and smiling takes less energy and feels so much better.

4. Positivity breeds positivity. I needed people around me who were driven and goal orientated. I needed people who would help lift my spirits just like I would help lift theirs. I had a new state of mind. If you couldn't provide, not materialistically, but as a whole contribute a smile or a laugh, then step aside. Four resolutions. Not so bad for my first time. I didn't want to overwhelm myself.

******

I started receiving my blessings the day I arrived in Atlanta. I loved my apartment. I felt a sense of freedom and relief. A'vern was one of the first people I met. Ironically, he was from Texas, Houston though not Dallas. He was a gay male, 30 years old, 5'7" 140 pounds, toned body, caramel complexion, long dreadlocks and a winning smile. His demeanor was amazing. He was warm and seemed very trustworthy. I immediately felt connected to him, and I told him I was almost carjacked, robbed and beaten. It was like I'd known him my entire life. He was a gay brother. He listened to the story and could relate to what I was talking about. He showed so much concern, and his face looked so stunned. I knew it was a lot to take in , but he was very empathetic. I felt very comfortable with him. He was easy to talk to. He gave me a big hug when I was done. I knew he'd be a friend to keep.

Our first Friday night together was spent at "Rain" a nightclub in downtown Atlanta. It was beautiful. This had to be the biggest club I had ever been to. It was huge. I loved it. There were all kinds of men all over. I knew Atlanta was the Black gay capital, but I had no idea there were so many. The club was packed. I was not looking for a man, but I sure enjoyed the scenery. I even ran into a few people from Roosevelt High School in Gary. It was a nice way to break into the new city. A'vern was super cool. The party was live, and I felt completely free.

The next day I planned to have dinner with James. He was one of the guys I "Requested" on *Facebook* in order to meet new people in Atlanta. James was one of the people who accepted. He said we should have dinner. I agreed. I met him and his friend Deon at Chow Baby's, a restaurant in Atlanta. James was 5'7", 150 pounds, he wore fitted clothes and his body was thick. He had on light makeup and was a little more feminine than I expected. It made me nervous. The hostess sat us in the middle of the floor where everyone could see. I was trying to work on my appearance and the perception that people had of me. I didn't want to stand out and make a scene. But James was warm, welcoming, and lovable. He was very feminine, but he didn't make it uncomfortable for me or the people around us. His friend, Deon, was dark brown skin, 5'9 and slim. He was a cool dude. He didn't say too much. He was the perfect complement to James. They were like Ying and Yang.

I had three new associates and new surroundings. I wanted to forget about Dallas, but I couldn't. Physical therapy three times a week was a constant reminder. My right finger was broken and my wrist was sprained. I had to go. My therapist was a sweet black woman from Atlanta. She made therapy as pleasant as it could be, I guess, but the reason I was there was always at the front of my mind.

******

Mina gave me until January to get settled. By February, she was ready to talk book business. The original book was gone. Price took the laptop one night after a fight. I was going to have to start from scratch. The book was the main reason I was in Atlanta. I was completely fine with that. We had a meeting to go over guidelines and standards. What was on *Facebook* was good. In order to make it a book, I would have to dig deeper and expose more. I was ready to expose it all. I'd been through the fire, crawled through a bed of razors, and swam across an alcohol river. I knew I wasn't the only person who took that trip. I was sure that many people had and only few made it to the other side. I was one of the few. I wanted to make sure no one else had to take a journey so horrible. Or if they were already on that path, maybe I could be an inspiration to change. I survived the valley and was walking into the sunshine. I wanted to help as many people get out the valley or avoid it all together, as I could. Mina said when I finished my draft she and one of her editors would read through the book and make any necessary corrections. The thought of sharing my story with, not just strangers, but the world, was heavy. I wanted to make sure it was delivered with integrity and conviction. My mind was flooded. I started writing as soon as I got home. I was still in physical therapy.

I couldn't type. I was jotting things down in my notebook. Let the journey begin.

I was keeping my gay friends to a minimum. A'vern, James, and Deon were enough. I'd been burnt too many times and didn't want too many gay friends in Atlanta. Gay men are like women. They gossip too much and love to start drama. I wanted straight friends, no DL dudes. Just straight niggas who smoked, chilled, and respected me like I would re spect them. I was on a new kick— no hair, and I cut my nails. I was less feminine. I was trying to listen to more Rap and make myself stand out even less. Tee was a straight up nigga. He knew a good connect and came through to blow down on a regular. I was helping him and his girl out until they got a car. She needed a ride to work and to be picked up. I didn't have a problem with that.

A'vern and I were together all the time. You could say he was like a best friend. Certain people I met never left my side. A'vern was one of them. In February, we hit up a new club "91." He'd never been and of course I hadn't, so it was going to be interesting. The line was long, but everyone looked young. When we finally got inside, it was one huge room crawling with infants. I was immediately put off. I figured we paid to get in so I might as well try and have a good time. That wasn't going to happen. The place was wack. I was high when I walked in, and it was blown in no time.

A'vern was having a good time though. He met a boy. They were talking for a while, but as soon as the conversation was wrapped, I told him it was time to go. I had plans the next morning. This club was not worth me being late or tired.

Facebook was vital in my quest to find friends. I knew a few people from Gary were in Atlanta. Then I found Keisha. We went to high school together. We were cool because she was a lesbian, and I was gay. That was no longer the case. She was now married and had a son when I went to go visit her in Snellville. We were crying before we even hugged. She looked so good and happy. It was such a pleasant visit. We talked about life, what changed in the last 15 years, and what stayed the same. It was wonderful seeing her and her beautiful son.

******

"Yo, where'd you get your car painted?"

I was at the gas pump when I turned around. This fine, 5'9" redbone brother was talking to me. I had to gain my composure. He was asking me about the racing strips on the car. I didn't know what to tell him. Price got the car painted. So that's what I said, minus the husband part.

"My homeboy knew someone and got it done for me."

"Yeah, that's clean, the black and white like that. I like it. I'm Skillz."

"I'm Samuel."

We spoke a minute. I didn't tell him I was gay, and he didn't ask.

I knew he wasn't though, shucks. He was a Georgia native, real cool. His car was nice, one of those big old school convertibles, made me think of the movie Thelma and Louis. He asked me if I smoked. Weed was a universal unifier. We exchanged numbers, and he came by the house later. He showed up with a bottle. I liked that. Never go to anyone's house empty handed. I wasn't providing for anyone but me, unless the person was contributing. Skillz was a producer. He didn't have one girl he had many friends. He was cool as hell. We smoked, threw a couple drinks back, chilled and talked. Tee came through and matched another blunt. It was a cool night.

March 7th I woke up to a highly unexpected phone call from Price. I hadn't spoken to him since December. He wanted me to know that he moved back to Chicago. I didn't care. Why would I care? He was going on and on about himself mentioned nothing about me. He didn't ask how I was. He wanted me to care about him but had no concern for me. Those days were long gone. He did ask me the guy's name that beat me. I told him the name I knew, but I didn't know the boy, he did. The conversation started to go sour, and I hung up. I didn't have time for foolishness.

I was writing in the book when "Skillz" called. He told me his dog had puppies, and there was one he could get rid of and asked if I wanted it. I was not a dog fan. I already had Tabby so I declined. He said it was cool and asked me if I wanted to come over and chill. I was having writers block and needed to back away from the book for a moment. So I went over. I think he set me up because as soon as I walked in this cute little black and white puppy was all over me. I sat on the couch. She jumped in my lap and wanted to lick my face. She was the cutest thing. Skillz pointed out that there was an "M" on the top of her head. I laughed and called her "Mariah". After that she had to come home with me. I was falling in love with her big puppy eyes. I named her so I had to take her home. I had a new puppy. I was so happy. I was nervous to bring her in the house. I didn't know how Tabby would respond to a dog in the house. Surprisingly, they got along fine. When Mariah came in, Tabby sniffed her. They had animal talk, I guess, and we all fell asleep on the couch.

I was going to Minnesota at the end of the month to evict my tenant. I was down to one house, and she was trashing it. I couldn't have that. I wasn't working at all, and I couldn't. I was considered disabled. Plus I was working on my book, and I needed to focus.

I needed the money I got from my house, and my rental property was my only income. A'vern agreed to watch the house and feed Tabby while I was gone. "Skillz" kept Mariah for me, and I left for Minnesota.

It was business as soon as I landed. I went to the house and made sure the tenant that was being evicted was gone and started preparing for the new one. My girls Michelle, Jasmine, Crystal and Molly came over. We made a party out of it, painting the walls, and hanging closet doors scrubbing toilets and counters. There was so much trash. She had a dog, contrary to the lease. It pissed all on the carpet and left stains. We had to shampoo the floor three times before the smell was gone. It was hard work, but at the end of the day the house was as immaculate as it was the day I got it. I moved the new tenant in and chilled for the rest of the weekend. Grandma Hazel was turning 75 years old, and they were having a party for her. Everyone was there. It was drama free with cake and good food. We had a good time. All good things must come to an end. On April 6th, I was on a flight back to Atlanta. Time to get back to my book!

******

The next morning I received a call from Texas Victim Crimes. I was working with them and the police to get the men arrested and to get my medical bills paid. The woman on the phone said my claim was being denied because I didn't live in the state of Texas. The fund was only for Texas residents. There was some sort of mix up because I was a Texas resident when it happened, but I wasn't going to stay there. Someone attempted to murder me. She told me I needed to come back to Texas and speak with the police and supervising officials because they were dropping my case. I had five days. Texas was a ten hour drive, and I really didn't want to do it alone.

We left at two o'clock in the morning on April 13th. I was happy I didn't have to take the journey alone. It was going to be a turn-around trip. Talk to the people I needed to talk to and leave the next afternoon. We played Keisha Cole, and I sang the entire trip. Red Bulls kept me going. I drove straight through. We arrived in Texas late afternoon. I didn't want to rush the time I was allowed with the police and Texas Victim Crimes, so I decided we'd go straight to the hotel and do that in the morning. Damion came over as soon as we got there. It was good to see him. It had been four months, but we talked just about every day. He was on a lunch break. So I took him back to work, and I drove into downtown Dallas for lunch. After work Damion came back, and we chilled the entire night.

I woke up early the next morning and went to handle my business. I had all the information I needed, and the process was smooth and easy. They told me they were going to review the case again. I should hear something within 30 days. I went back to the hotel to grab A'vern and drove over to Damion's to say our goodbyes. I had no desire to stay in Dallas. Business was finished. It was time to go. This time I might as well have been driving alone. A'vern slept the entire ride back, but I was okay. I had my Keisha Cole CD, and A'vern introduced me to a few songs from Kayne West's CD, "*Twisted Dark Fantasies.*" I was rolling. We got home around four o'clock in the morning, and I was exhausted. I thanked A'vern for keeping me company, and we parted ways.

April 21st, made a year that I'd been separated from Price. I wanted to celebrate. I wanted to celebrate hard. A'vern said he'd go out with me, so we went to Bulldog's. It wasn't my first choice for a club, but the 21st fell on a Thursday. I wanted to go out that night, so Bulldog's it was. The club was packed with boys, boys and more boys. We had a blast. My mind was free, and I was too. There was nothing left but to dance, dance, dance.

******

The new car thing was weighing heavily on my mind. At the top of May, I saw a Kia in the mall parking lot and B-lined straight to the dealership. They had several models, but the one that piqued my interest was the 2011

Optima Turbo. The car was clean, mature and sexy, just like me. I had to have it. I traded the Mitsubishi Gallant and drove my brand new baby off the lot. I named her "Accomplished" because I knew that's where I was heading. A'vern posted a picture on *Facebook* and tagged me in it. This was one of the best and worst things that could've happened. My mom, with whom I hadn't spoken to in months, called me and asked me for money. A few cousins sent messages on *Facebook* asking me for money. Everyone thought I was rich because I lived in Atlanta and had a new car. Even if I had it certain people would never get it. Period. I wasn't looking out for leeches. If you could not provide, step aside.

Writing the book was becoming more of a challenge. Some of the topics were really painful, and I found myself crying and losing focus often. I had a meeting with Mina, and she stressed we needed to meet a deadline, June 28th, that way the book would be out by summer's end like we wanted. I told her it was becoming more and more difficult, but I would try and meet the deadline.

I spoke to my father's cousin "Aunt" Ann in mid-May. She was the first person from my dad's side to take a trip to Minnesota to see me. She made me proud to be a part of the family. She and her family were coming to Atlanta for the weekend, and she wanted to see me. I didn't really know my father's siblings or my cousins but I wanted to, so I agreed to meet them. We went to P.F. Chang's for dinner. I never ate there before. I was hoping it would be something I wanted. Aunt Ann's two children, Tori and Demetrius, were there along with Tori's children. We talked about everything. I felt so comfortable with them. It was like the time spent apart didn't matter. We were family, and that was it. I was invited to attend church with them. I had not been since I arrived in Atlanta. I wanted to go, so I went. The sermon was lovely and uplifting just like the time spent with my family. I hated that they had to go, but there was word of a family reunion Fourth of July weekend, and I planned to be in attendance.

I buckled down in June. I had to get the first draft finished. It was hard. But I was getting it done. Ironically, while I was on the chapters pertaining to my husband and me, he called. He was remorseful. He apologized repeatedly and said he never meant for what happened to happen. He never wanted me dead and loved me so much. I didn't know where any of it was coming from.

I accepted his apology, but it didn't really mean anything to me. I didn't feel connected to him anymore. I loved him but not the same way. I had to get off the phone. I had something more pressing to handle.

******

Deadline was met, and now it was time to hang with the Holloways. I drove to Charlotte, North Carolina the morning of July 2nd. My dad and all of his siblings were at Aunt Mary's house when I arrived. My cousins were also there, and the smell of good Bar-B-Que was floating through the air. My father was "looking good." I was happy to see him. It had been almost a year. My cousins and I caught up on life. The last time I saw everyone was at my grandfather's funeral, so there was a lot of catching up to do. We slept in North Carolina. Early Saturday the entire house caravanned to Aunt Katt's house in Cowpen, South Carolina. My cousins Marcellus and Marcus were going to be there. I couldn't wait to see them. Marcus went to school with me, so I knew him. I loved getting to know my family. Knowing someone made me feel much more comfortable. The weekend was amazing. I thanked GOD for all my blessings. I was alive and it felt excellent.

I chilled for a while because the last week in July was going to be busy. I was taking a road trip to the North. My best friend BJ was getting married, and I was one of the groomsmen.

One o'clock Thursday morning, I started my ten-hour journey to Gary, Indiana. I was going to see my dad, aunts, cousins and friends since I was going to be in the area. I arrived at my dad's around two o'clock in the evening. I was so tired and happy to see him. I hadn't been to Gary in over a year. There was so much to do, and I was only going to be there for a day and a half. I saw everyone I could that day, including my father. Chicago was only 20 minutes outside of Gary. Price and his mother wanted me to visit, I was nervous. This was the first time I would see Price since the hospital in Dallas. I pulled up in front of the house and Price came outside. His mother wasn't home, but that was okay I'd just come back to see her. He wanted to take to me to dinner, so we went to Ray's Shrimp House. Shrimp and fries was the order, just one that we shared. He wanted to talk too, mostly about us. I wasn't interested. I was happy to see him. He looked good, and I was happy he was well. That was the extent of it. I wasn't interested in being with him, not a lot or a little. I loved myself too much to take all those steps backwards. I wasn't bitchy about it though. I told him straight up and kept a smile. We enjoyed the rest of our food, and I dropped him off at home.

On the way back to Gary, I thought about Price. It was funny. He kept saying he was ready to come home, like he was in jail or on vacation. He felt like he could just come back into my life at any moment. No the grass was not greener on the other side, and he wasn't getting anywhere near my green grass. It was behind a locked "face." I crashed as soon as I got to Michial's house. I was so tired!

Early the next morning I got a call from Price. He wanted to go to breakfast. I liked to eat and still had to see his mother and aunt, so I went. Scrambled eggs, sausage and toast that was the normal order when we hit up Daily's Diner. I guess he thought I'd change the way I felt if I knew more about what he was going through. He said he learned how hard it was to live in this world. Financial stability was a hard place to reach, and he really knew what it was like to take care of himself. He didn't want to be in Chicago. There was nothing there for him. I didn't know what to say. I was happy he was maturing, but I didn't have room in my life for him. I loved him, but I no longer wanted him. It was that simple. We went back to his mother's house. She was finally home. His aunt was there too. We talked it up a while, took some pictures and I had to make moves. I had a wedding to attend the next day that was five hours away in Wisconsin. I still had people to see, and I needed to get ready for the road.

I stopped through and said bye to everyone before I left and was on my way to Wisconsin. BJ was getting married. I was excited for my friend. He was 28 years old; the same age I was when I got married. I prayed his marriage would be blissful and blessed. I arrived 15 minutes late for the rehearsal, but I made it and after watching the run through I knew this was going to be a match made in heaven. On July 24, 2010, my best friend of 12 years got married. BJ and Ashley had one of the most diverse weddings I'd ever attended. I was happy to be a part of it. I partied my butt off. I did all of my favorite hustles from the Electric Slide to the Cupid Shuffle and even The Wobble. I had a ball! I didn't want to leave, but I had another five-hour drive to Minnesota. I needed to check on my tenant, see my family then head back to Gary to pick up Angela and then to Atlanta.

******

On the road to Atlanta with my best friend Angela, it was a beautiful day. I was tired and hadn't been to sleep in almost 24 hours with ten hours of road still in front me. It was cool. Even if Angela went to sleep, I had Beyoncé, Keisha and Mary, plus a few Red Bulls to keep me company. Angela stayed awake and we talked the entire trip. We covered new topics, refreshed old ones and talked about the realities that weren't so far into the future. It was a nice drive, and even nicer when I was looking at my front door. I made it to the bed, and that was all she wrote.

Wednesday was chill. I took Angela sightseeing and shopping. It was nice having her so close. We maxed out the day, I slept even harder that night. By Thursday I was fully recovered and ready to show Angela a good time. I was going to make dinner and A'vern, James and Deon were coming over. We smoked well and ate better. We wanted to go clubbing and decided upon Bull Dogs. Angela went upstairs in sweats and returned in a sexy miniskirt and pumps. I put on jean shorts, a button down and polo sneakers; A'vern, James and Deon were just as dapper. We loaded into the car and headed to the club. The line was long as usual meaning it was packed inside. When we walked in, I was on a cloud both mentally and spiritually. We hit the dance floor and I closed my eyes thanking GOD for his graciousness and the strength that kept me alive. I exhaled a sigh of relief.

I was 32 and finally loved me. I was free. I let the joy from my heart pour out my feet, and I danced, I danced and smiled with people who truly loved me!!

THE END

So…
Some said I couldn't do it;
Some said I wouldn't amount to anything,
But I never let that take away my pride.
I never let it kill my dreams.

Many tried to scare me. It's only GOD I fear.
After many trials, roadblocks, and dead ends,
I'm still here.

1 time I tried to take it all away
with suicide on my mind—
No more tears, no more pain.

7 years without some family to accept me because I was gay
With new friends I held on strong day after day

3 years of love with that special one to laugh, and cry with
He shared his family, he shared his heart.

Add it all up
After 11 long years, take a look at me
Do you see some of me in you?

Now come try walking in my shoes…

Lightning Source UK Ltd.
Milton Keynes UK
UKOW06f1114180516

274496UK00001B/177/P